DUNCAN DANCE

DUNCAN DANCE ∼

A Guide For Young People Ages Six to Sixteen

Julia Levien

With illustrations by the author from life and memory

A Dance Horizons Book
Princeton Book Company, Publishers

A Dance Horizons Book
Princeton Book Company, Publishers
P.O. Box 57
Pennington, New Jersey 08534

Cover art by Julia Levien
Cover design by Frank Bridges and Connie Woodford
Interior design by Donna Wickes

Library of Congress Cataloging-in-Publication Data

Levien, Julia.
    Duncan Dance : a guide for young people ages six to sixteen /
Julia Levien.
        p. cm.
    "A Dance Horizons book."
    Includes index.
    ISBN 0-87127-198-2
    1. Modern Dance. 2. Duncan, Isadora, 1877–1927. I. Title.
GV1783.L45 1994
792.8—dc20   94–38228

CONTENTS ॐ

PREFACE

The effect of Isadora Duncan on the development of the art of the dance has been generally acknowledged. But the realization of her important contribution to the field of education for children through the dance is still to be fully appreciated. In 1904, when Isadora announced her free school for the "New Dance," most of her suggestions, which today are unquestioned, were unheard of. Her school, open to all children from all economic levels, advocated the arts as an integral part of the curriculum and that children should experience their body through dance movements as an avenue to learning. The school allowed for life with untrammeled bodies in sandaled feet as well as time to meditate. All these were new concepts.

By 1907, the philosopher Rudolf Steiner and the musician Emile Jaques-Dalcroze had established their own schools, which featured movement in education. Meanwhile, Maria Montessori, a pioneer educator, was advocating education as a right of every child, even those from the working class. In 1914, George Bernard Shaw wrote *Pygmalion*, a play intended to show that the differences between the street waif and the grand lady could be eliminated with proper cultural education.

The opening of the Isadora Duncan School in Grunewald, Berlin, in 1904 predated all of these efforts. When Isadora and her sister, Elizabeth, created their live-in school, it was indeed the beginning of a new era in education. Isadora was at the forefront there, even as she was in the art of the dance. Writers of that period such as John Galsworthy and Upton Sinclair wrote enthusiastically about the school. And the prominent artists de Segonzac, Bourdelle, and Denis recorded their images from classes there, recognizing the timelessness of Isadora's message.

The following lessons were gleaned from my own experience, as well as from my observations of children's dance classes of the Elizabeth Duncan School, which periodically carried on classes in New York. For many years I was associated with both Anna Duncan and Irma Duncan, who were from the original Duncan School in Berlin. I worked with them as a teacher as well as performing in their independent dance companies. The classwork is from material accumulated over many years of association with this first generation of Isadora's disciples and from my subsequent time as an independent artist. I do feel that children of today's unsettled world will still find this dance not only relevant but also restorative.

Duncan's ideas on children dancing have been collected in her published writings, *Art of the Dance*; yet, today, little is known of her actual process of teaching. Her approach was not only inspirational, it also supplied specific patterns for learning movement. As a basic language of the dance it shaped the "new dance" that she believed would lead to universal communication and to a better world.

Many of Isadora Duncan's ideas on "natural movement" have been absorbed into the field of contemporary dance therapy. However, today's emphasis by dance schools on the disciplines of classical ballet for the training of professionals to supply the many growing ballet companies has limited the opportunity for the dance, as part of education, to be part of art in life. There needs to be a dance education that is relevant to the public-at-large—that is, to the people. Only then can we hope to realize Isadora's vision of seeing children everywhere, holding hands in circles, dancing a "Reigen"—in a world of peace, "the highest intelligence in the freest body" (Duncan, from *Art of the Dance*).

Julia Levien

ACKNOWLEDGMENTS

This difficult project would probably never have been completed without the assistance and encouragement of a host of well-wishers and practical helpers, as I groped my way to firm-footed reality. Although I have taught Duncan's dance over a considerable period of time, the formulization of all this heritage of creative energy appeared like an illusive fantasy. All the needed words seemed to dance capriciously in my head, but were wary of settling down into print. So, I am indeed appreciative of those who guided and goaded me into what I hope is an acceptable form, worthy of the precious material of this Duncan dance legacy.

In the very beginning, there were all those who let themselves be subjected to my first faltering attempts to find a suitable creative formula: the first, brave Mary Jo Fenio (who also typed these final sentences); the summer of '93 dance workshop of Carolyn Adams of the Paul Taylor Dance Company and her co-worker Julie Strandberg; then later, responsive Lori Belilove and her performing company; Karen Dantzler, Cherlyn Smith, Jennifer Sprowl, Margaret Velez; in addition, there were the former members of the Isadora Commemorative Dance Company—Judy Landon and Adrienne Ramm, as well as Jodi Liss.

Many thanks for the good will and help of my colleagues Hortense Kooluris and Louise Craig Gerber as well as my dear friend Elaine Babian. My gratitude for the fortitude and devotion of Therese Anne Joseph who typed from my mysterious handwriting, and connected me to the help of the Charlotte Koch Foundation, and my appreciation of the tenacity of David Ramm who turned it all into almost well-behaved type—in recognizable sequential shapes.

Most of all thanks to my all-seeing editors—Barbara Palfy, who navigated me firmly through the highs and lows of endless passages, and Debi Elfenbein, who kept the light of the goal visible, a beacon in a boundless sea.

A few words about the illustrations. Although not trained specifically as a professional pictorial artist, I have been sketching and sculpting the dance image almost all of my life. Since there was no camera fast enough to completely catch the motion of dance at the height of the Duncan dance influence, it was a necessary challenge to me to bring out of memory and re-creation the fleeting moments so important in visualizing the high points of transition in action. My intent has been to fasten the image to the page for the guidance of the student and the teacher.

May this little guidebook serve its purpose, "Where the feet go—there goes the future." —Isadora Duncan, 1902

In conclusion, a special thanks to the combined efforts of all those who helped in the creation of the companion video record of technique and choreography of the Duncan Dance: Andrea Seidel, who directed the young talented members of the Duncan Dance Ensemble with the cooperation of Daniel Lewis, Dean of Dance, New World School of the Arts of Miami; and the assistance of the DanceArts Foundation, Inc.

All of this, of course, would not be possible without the fore-sightedness and understanding of my publisher, Charles Woodford.

Dedicated to the Memory
of my Mother
Rashel Weprinsky
who led me to find the path to Isadora's Dance
and my wonderful dance teachers
Anna Duncan
and
Irma Duncan
who kept me on that path.

INTRODUCTION

Freedom, flow and spontaneity are the keys to the quality of movement in the Duncan Dance. To achieve these qualities requires self-discipline as well as a heightened sense of self-awareness. Duncan, in shaping this art, took from the nature of universal peoples those movements common to all, such as walking, running, and skipping, to build a vocabulary for the basis of the new dance.

This is especially evident in the movements of children, as Isadora noted. She hoped that this dance would reach them before a disruptive society had denied them their birthright—the right to grow in harmony with themselves and their fellow beings.

To recognize the values in great visual arts is also part of the necessary learning experience. To appreciate line and form is essential in the understanding of all art. In this dance there is an aesthetic that should be part of a social culture, a communicating, interacting art form, which is at the same time an instrument for better education.

Until this concept of dance is used not only for corrective physical therapy, but also as an intrinsic part of our early and ongoing education system, this little guidebook hopes to remind the dancing body of Duncan's rediscovery of the right to positive assertion and the joy of action.

The role of music is one of the basic and unique approaches to the awakening of dance response. The lessons are best when accompanied at the piano by a musical artist. The dance studies need to be coordinated with the music to create an artistic atmosphere for rhythmic and imaginative responses. The student is encouraged to listen and react quickly. The musician does not follow the dancer. The music listed here was used in the Duncan schools, but the musician should feel free to use suitable alternatives or improvise accordingly. If taped music is used, be careful that repetition does not lead to rote.

It is essential that the dance movements should appear spontaneous, not become mechanical. The study patterns using basic movements help to avoid this. The music itself must spark the freshness of action.

The legs and feet are the pulse and motor following the well-defined rhythm. This can range over the variety of steps, from a smoothly sliding waltz to a bouncing polka. The arms and upper body follow the melodic phrase, dancing with gestures to an imagined scene or a real partner. What emerges is a truly creative process that gives a great deal of freedom within the demands of the form. Each student discovers and rediscovers this element of dance with more and more confidence.

It must be emphasized that every movement emerges both physically and emotively from the body center—the "solar plexus"—and then radiates outward to become part of the surrounding space, both immediate and limitless. To spring up from the floor acknowledges the earth that holds in itself the pull of gravity. The upward thrust opposes this; the descent holds back as it yields.

"That each action must have an equal and opposite reaction" was part of our learning the laws of nature.

SLOW MOVEMENTS

1

In the slow movements are the essentials of the Duncan approach to finding the original impulses of motives relating to motion. "All movements must start from the center," Isadora taught. That "center" is located physically in what we call the "solar plexus." Anatomically, it is the muscle belt of the diaphragm, which controls the breath and reacts, both by expanding positively and contracting negatively, according to the variety of emotions imposed on it. From this awareness, Duncan developed a rational sense of primal body movement as well as arm and hand gestures that radiate from this inner core of energy, liberating the disciplined body into a cycle of ongoing and renewed wavelike energy: the movement that starts from within, emanates from the center to its direction, and then goes outward for infinite renewal. Music supplies the emotional springboard for this "motor-charged" movement of Duncan dancing for students of all ages. The sequence that creates the special style of dance emerges: first the idea and the music, then the thought and emotion, then the movement and the dance.

PREPARATORY EXERCISES

Releasing Arms and Body (curl and uncurl)

MUSIC   Any Brahms intermezzo or similar adagio.

STARTING
POSITION   Stand with the feet together, heels touching, toes out. Place right hand in front over the solar plexus area. Fingers touch lightly the area between the sternum and waist. Place left hand on the back directly opposite, feel the spine center.

DESCRIPTION   Bend forward from the waist, rounding over into "hairpin" position (Figure 1.1). Release both arms to hang relaxed, fingers toward toes. Bounce the body up and down, gently shake shoulders, release the head by shaking it. Lift the body slowly, push up against the backbone. Stretch the arms high overhead, open the hands. Change.

Drop arms slowly as body bends forward and inward. Curve in, move down until hands touch the floor. Remain down for a few seconds. Repeat lift and drop several times until the body begins to take on its own weighted release.

1.1 *"Hairpin" position.*

Rotating the Head

STARTING
POSITION   Place fingers on shoulders held down, keep neck free. Elbows stay down at side to keep shoulders still. Stand erect.

DESCRIPTION Rotate head and chin fully, chin to chest then around. Repeat twice in each direction. Breathe deeply.

Body Swings (Torso Swing from Side to Side)

STARTING POSITION Stand with feet well apart, toes out. Shift weight over to right foot, extend left foot to side. Lift both arms high overhead on right side. Turn body, chest faces to the side. Look up at hands (Figure 1.2).

DESCRIPTION Slowly drop weight of arms down and around. At the same time move body and arms down and over to the front. Tuck hips under curved body, bend both knees. Pause. Shift weight over to left foot, come up slowly to left. Straighten left knee, turn chest to left, look up (see Figure 1.2), lift body, stretch arms up and overhead. Continue to swing the trunk down and up in an arc eight to ten times.

1.2 *Starting position.*

Rotating the Trunk

STARTING POSITION Place feet a good distance apart, toes turned out. Relax arms at side.

DESCRIPTION Bend forward from waist, hang loose down.

Complete a rotation to the left. Keep arms down
at sides. Move from the waist first down to the
front, then to left side, bending knees as chest
moves from the side to arch back. Release head,
push hips forward as back bends to arch. Continue to the right. Contract inward during
forward bend. Pause. Repeat rotation. Do two
consecutive rotations in each direction.

After each exercise, release over forward.
Stand quietly, breathe deeply.

BASIC ARM MOVEMENTS

Slow

MUSIC Chopin preludes, nocturnes, or similar adagios.

STARTING
POSITION Stand with heels touching, weight forward. Arms
released at sides, elbows turned out, fingers
extended.

DESCRIPTION As the music begins, close the eyes for a few
seconds and listen. When ready to start, at first
feel the energy rising from the center, the solar
plexus. Respond to the music, letting the arms
feel very light. First lift the chest, then the upper
arms begin to lift. Fingers feel the weight of
gravity pulling downward, arms oppose the pull
smoothly (Figure 1.3a). Gradually the entire arms
are lifted outward and the chest has pushed up
from the start as both arms have moved together
by the response to the musical cadence — a
primal movement emerges, as if into light. At the
height of the shoulders, pause. Breathe deeply.

Start to bring the arms down slowly with a
reversal of hand position from palms down to
palms out (Figure 1.3b). Elbows lead the movement until hands touch sides.

Resume arm movement upward by starting to
raise the elbows. Lift up against gravity, descend
by opposing the effort from high. Repeat several
times.

1.3 *Basic movements.*

Gestures to Earth, Self, Universe

MUSIC — Chopin preludes, nocturnes, or similar adagios.

STARTING POSITION — Stand with feet together, toes slightly turned out. Weight on right foot. Arms at sides. Younger children in circle face center, older students scatter places face front to teacher, mirror image.

DESCRIPTION — Begin with the right arm alone. Bend forward

1.4 *Gesture to the universe.*

slightly. Look down, see the earth and growing things. Gesture with the right hand toward the space directly in front of the feet. Shift weight over to the left foot. Move the hand with the wrist leading (Figure 1.5a).

Bring the right elbow up. Raise the arm slowly until the hand touches the center of the chest, fingers turned in, wrist bent. Look down, sense the energy within the self (Figure 1.5b).

Turn the face to look up. Lift the right arm with bent elbow leading. Raise the chest up at the same time with a deep breath (Figure 1.5c). Continue to raise the right arm up overhead until the arm is stretched fully. Feel the ongoing tension throughout the body. Stretch upward out of the self. Release the energy past the hand (Figure 1.5d).

Bring the right arm out to the side, palm up. Pause with the arm at shoulder level, still looking up. Turn the head to look at the outstretched hand (Figure 1.5e). Take a small breath, turn the palm down, lower the arm slowly. Keep the elbow rounded. Look down. Return arm to side. Center the weight again.

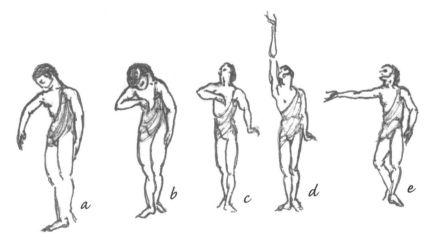

1.5 *Slow movements—arm gestures.*

Repeat the action with the left arm. Then with both arms together. Focus before moving.

To create the gesture "to the universe," make a large circular movement with both arms. Look down, arms crossed, then within, then look up and lift out. When both arms are held out at the apex of the outward gesture, keep the face up. Pause, with the palms turned up. Feel expanded, fully released (Figure 1.6). Slowly turn the palms down. Bring both arms down to the sides. Look down. Center the weight again.

1.6 *Gestures: (a) to earth; (b) to self; (c) from self; (d) to space; (e) to universe*

RECLINING AND RISING

MUSIC   Liszt, "Liebestraum," or Chopin nocturnes.

STARTING   In center of the space, face front, feet together.
POSITION   Stand lightly, look down, think of an inviting place to lie down and rest.

DESCRIPTION When the music begins, connect to the sound, create a response that provokes a suitable motor energy. Step slowly and gently over to the right with the right foot, move diagonally. Curve the back over slightly, bring arms out to side, look down at side. Create each changing image mentally and react emotionally before moving. Then move with the legato music, guided by the phrases.

First look to the right side. Then look to the left in front of center (Figure 1.7a).

Sink slowly into the left knee, curve forward, both arms balance out to the sides. Crouch down. Kneel. Look into the described space of earth (Figure 1.7b).

Change weight over to left, place left hand on floor to the side. Sit sideward on left hip, left foot tucked under in back, right knee up. Look down and to the left. Move right arm out away from the body and out high to the right. Look up past right hand (Figure 1.7c). Stretch left arm out to left side on floor. Slowly lower the body. Slide lower and lower until completely down to the side. At the same time move the right arm in a half circle overhead to the left, with eyes following until the head is resting on the shoulder face down. Rest right arm over head across left with palm down (Figure 1.7d). After a brief repose start to rise slowly as if drawn by a magnet. Turn head to right, face to side (Figure 1.7e). Sit up, raise right arm out to side. Look down in front. Rise up onto left knee. Raise both arms out to side (Figure 1.7f). Look up. Leave right knee out, relaxed to the side. Pause (Figure 1.7g).

Move right knee over to the front of body. Bend forward over right knee, push back leg up to raise body to hairpin fold-in, arms crossed in front of body. Hands touch the ground (Figure 1.7h). Slowly straighten up, unfold the body. Lift the arms up from crossed position into the opening "gesture to the universe" (Figure 1.7i).

1.7 *Lying down and rising.*

TWO "TANAGRA FIGURES"

The "Tanagra figures" are done especially to sense a smooth transfer of the body weight from one image to another. The student should seek to sustain the line and proper placement.

MUSIC   Corelli, "Theme and Variations"

TIME   3/4, adagio. Count four measures of three beats each for each change of gesture image. Move slowly.

Running Tanagra

STARTING POSITION   Before starting, practice transfer of weight from foot to foot, bringing heel off the floor. Then stand still, heels together, arms at side. Move weight onto left foot, right knee and foot relaxed (Figure 1.8a).

DESCRIPTION   *measures one–four:* Image one—raise both arms forward to shoulder height, wrists held loosely, hands parallel, drop head forward. At the same time raise right knee up forward with foot hanging loosely toward the floor (Figure 1.8b).

measures five–eight: Image two—relevé (lift up) on left foot, bring right knee and foot over to right side. Drop weight onto right foot, softly. At the same time raise both hands over to right. Right hand is held higher than left, palm out, left arm over chest, palm out. Look back over left shoulder (Figure 1.8c). This movement is taken from images in Renaissance paintings and drawings depicting movement of running away, caught in a frame of one moment.

1.8 *Tanagra figures—running.*

measures nine—twelve: Image three—bring weight back to left foot, draw right foot back. Bring both arms high up overhead. Look straight ahead, stand erect (Figure 1.8d).

measures thirteen—sixteen: Image four—return hands to sides, heels come together.

Repeat entire sequence to left.

Kneeling Tanagra

STARTING POSITION
: Stand with heels together, arms at sides.

DESCRIPTION
: *measures one–four:* Image one—look down beyond the right foot, bend over slightly (Figure 1.9a).

measures five–eight: Image two—step to diagonal right side, extend left leg behind. Stand with weight fully on right foot (Figure 1.9b).

measures nine–twelve: Image three—move. Lift left knee up, with small relevé on right foot (Figure 1.9c). Land lightly on left foot on the diagonal. Kneel on the right knee, bend over. Move right hand over in front of left foot. Gesture as if finding a precious object. Stretch left arm behind back to balance (Figure 1.9d).

measures thirteen–sixteen: Image four—stand up. Step forward on diagonal on right foot. Lift right hand high, palm up, to corner, head lifted as body rises from kneeling. Gesture as if holding object to light (Figure 1.9e).

1.9 *Tanagra figures—kneeling.*

measures seventeen—twenty: Image five—step back onto left foot, with a flow of weight slowly from left foot to right hand. Look back up at right hand (Figure 1.9f).

measures twenty-one—twenty-four: Image six—lower right arm slowly. Draw right foot in, feet together, arms at side. Look down. Finish by counting two measures, standing still.

Repeat entire sequence to the left side. Before moving, always look and focus.

BARRE WORK

2

Barre work, or *Beinschwingen*, as it is done in Duncan classes, is
essential and always consistent in its aims. Besides limbering and
stretching, it is the containment of the body's line and center—the
body learns its geography from head to toe. The important
attributes that Isadora gave to the center of gravity and its mobility
are made valid for every demand on it—both for its separateness
and for its wholeness. When lifting the legs, the power source will
be moved to bend the upper part of the hips, which results in a
longer line than the usual ballet barre gives. The arms must also
move as indicated in the lesson on Slow Movement, while the
body is always controlled from the center or solar plexus. The legs
extend from hip to toe in special alignment to the spine and pelvis,
in order to gather both strength and suppleness. Turnout is always
stressed but not carried to extremes.

Isadora extracted what she thought necessary from the ballet
barre, but she used a completely different approach to achieve an
inner discipline that would accommodate her concept of a new,
free, and volatile dance form. What emerges here, without help
from mirrors, is a self-image free of narcissism.

MUSIC   Johann Strauss or Schubert waltzes, or impro-
         visation.

TIME   3/4; tempos to suit action, accent on first beat.

STARTING
POSITION
Left hand lightly holding barre, stand at right angle to barre, heels touching, toes out to form a "V" shape of the feet. Pull buttocks under by tightening muscles. Knees turned out with the inner sides of the thighs touching. Hold head relaxed, shoulders down, chest at ease. Weight forward over balls of feet, back straight. Right hand down at side, fingers touch the side, elbow out.

DEEP KNEE BENDS (GRANDS PLIÉS)

TIME
Slow: two measures of three beats each for each change of image.

DESCRIPTION
measures one–two: Image one—lift chest, raise head, look straight ahead. Raise right arm out to shoulder level (move arm as described in Arm Movements) (Figure 2.1a). Rise high, weight centered firmly on balls of feet, push heels together. Stretch the inside of the arches well.

measures three–four: Image two—bend knees out to side, slowly lower body. Tuck buttocks under hips, back straight. Sit on heels, keep heels touching. Remain on half-toe, push knees out and downward. At the same time, bring right arm down to front from side. Point fingers down, turn elbow up. Look down at the space in front of feet (Figure 2.1b).

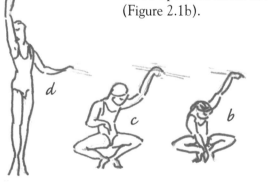

2.1 *Barre—deep knee bends.*

measures five–six: Image three—look up, lift right arm up, elbow first. Contract buttocks, lift body keep back straight. Move arm up while body is lifting (Figure 2.1c). Extend right arm high overhead, look way up. Stretch entire body from toes through fingertips. Keep palm facing in Breathe deeply (Figure 2.1d).

measures seven–eight: Image four—bring right arm out to side, then slowly down. Return to starting position.

Repeat entire sequence fast: one measure of three beats for each change of image, four times.

LEG LIFTS

Leg Lifts are more of a long, swinging lift of the leg than are battements or kicks. The entire leg begins to move with the lift from the thigh, similar to the way the upper arm lifts the hand. Fold the hips under the body while raising the leg. Lift the knee with the foot extended, knee relaxed. At the height of the lift straighten the knee. Swing the leg up hard, as high as possible up over the head. Lower the leg slowly to return the foot to the floor. Move the chest up and forward together with the leg lift. Lift the chest again on the step after the return. The legs should be extended and lifted as high as possible each time. Feel the hinge of the legs start from the upper part of the hips.

Leg Lift Forward

STARTING POSITION Left hand on barre, right arm out shoulder high, palm down, elbow out (see Figure 2.2a). Stand on right foot, weight fully back, left foot pointed front, stretched, heel well off the floor. Raise right arm high overhead (Figure 2.2b).

DESCRIPTION *measure one:* Step forward quickly onto left foot. Draw right foot forward, brushing along the floor. Keeping knee relaxed, swing right leg forward and up. Extend leg with foot pointed high overhead, look up. At the same time, swing right arm forward lightly. Keep left, supporting knee firm but not rigid (Figure 2.2c).

measure two: Bring right leg down slowly. Take large step back onto right foot, return to full weight. Keep knees relaxed. Extend left foot front, pointed. Lift chest, swing right arm down and back high to rear. Look back at lifted right hand. Straighten both knees.

Repeat six times with right leg forward as high as possible each time. Turn around to the left, right hand on barre. Bring left arm out to the side and lift left leg forward six times. Take two measures to turn around and resume the rhythm before starting with the alternate leg.

2.2 *Barre—leg lift forward.*

Leg Lift Side

Preparatory Exercise for Turnout (Tendu)

STARTING POSITION
Stand with heels touching, toes moderately turned out. Left hand on barre, right arm out to side, shoulder high.

DESCRIPTION
measure one: Extend right foot to side, stretch toes, arch, and ankle. Keep knee facing up. Feel hip turn out in line with foot. Heel under (Figure 2.3a).

measure two: Bring right foot in back of left, right instep touching heel of left foot (Figure 2.3b).

measure three: Extend right foot to side, stretch toes, arch, and ankle. Keep knee facing up. Feel hip turn out in line with foot. Heel under.

measure four: Bring right foot in front of left, right heel touching left instep (see Figure 2.3b).

Continue brushing the foot out and in to the side, alternating return back and front, eight times. Reverse: right hand on barre, work left foot.

Preparatory Exercise for Stretching the Arch (*Rond de Jambe*)

STARTING POSITION
Same as previous exercise.

DESCRIPTION
measure one: Point right foot front, heel up.

measure two: Point right foot side, heel under, knee up.

measure three: Point right foot back, heel under, knee out.

measure four: Slowly bring heels together, knee forward relaxed.

Reverse direction: back, side, front, together. Keep knees firm. Toes always brush the floor. Repeat for eight rotations, alternating direction, with each foot.

Leg Lift Side Completed

STARTING POSITION
Stand, right foot in back of left. Right arm out to side, shoulder high.

DESCRIPTION
measure one: Quickly raise right leg high and out to side, thigh first, knee soft and facing up. Bring knee up behind elbow. Look front, straighten knees. Hold leg high (Figure 2.3c).

measure two: Slowly lower right leg to front, heel first. Step with weight forward onto right foot, heel first, toes brushing. At the same time, move right arm and hand forward. Lift chest with a deep breath; look up at hand (Figure 2.3d).

2.3 Barre—to the side.

measure three: Again, raise right leg high out to the side, thigh first, knee up behind the elbow, out to side. Straighten the knees, point the toes. Hold the leg high (Figure 2.3e).

measure four: Slowly lower right leg to back. Step back onto the right foot, bring in heel first. Move right arm back, take a deep breath. Look up at right hand. Weight down on right foot in back (Figure 2.3f).

Repeat step forward, lift out, step back, lift out, for six side lifts right leg. Change to left leg. Always lift knee back of elbow.

Leg Lift Back

Preparatory Exercise (Relevé with Knee Lift)

STARTING POSITION Face barre, holding lightly with both hands. Arms extended while leaving enough space to lift the knee.

DESCRIPTION *measure one:* Lift right knee to chest. Rise to half-toe on left foot.

measure two: Lower to standing, flat heels together.

measure three: Lift left knee to chest. Rise to half-toe on right foot.

measure four: Lower to standing, heels together. Continue to repeat, alternating right and left.

Leg Swing with Arch

STARTING POSITION
Face barre, holding lightly with both hands. Stand on half-toe on left foot, right knee up in front. Look down at right knee, curve over forward (Figure 2.4a).

DESCRIPTION
measure one: Swing right leg back quickly: push thigh back, brush toe along the floor, foot back with knee bent out. Arch back and push head and shoulders back. Rise to half-toe on left foot. Relevé (Figure 2.4b).

measure two: Bring right leg down. Stand flat on both feet. Bring right knee up in front, rise to half-toe on left foot.

Continue to swing right knee and leg forward and

2.4 *Leg lift back arch.*

push back six times. Arch the back, try to reach foot to back of head.

Repeat with left knee and leg.

Leg Lift to Arabesque

STARTING POSITION
Face barre, holding lightly with both hands. Stand on both feet.

DESCRIPTION
measure one: Step forward on right foot, push hips toward the wall over right foot (Figure 2.5a).

measure two: Step back onto left foot, brush right foot back, swing right leg extended to the back, knee turned out, toes stretched. Arch back. Keep face up, chest lifted, shoulders even. Hold leg high in back, in line with head (Figure 2.5b).

measure three: Slowly return right foot to floor. Step forward onto right foot, push hips forward. Keep chest high, head straight.

measure four: Repeat right leg lift back to reach a good arch. Continue with right leg six more times. Pause. Change to left foot forward. Hold the eighth lift to finish with a high arch. Check alignment.

2.5 *Leg lift with arabesque.*

BODY FORWARD RELEASE AND BACK ARCH

STARTING POSITION
Place left hand on barre. Stand with feet well apart, right arm out at side.

DESCRIPTION
measure one: Drop body, bend in from waist, head down, fold over. Circle right arm out and down, hand down to toes, palm down. Touch floor with fingers, brushing past toes.

measure two: Keeping knees straight, lift the back up, raise arm with bent elbow. Stretch hand high up overhead. Look way up, stretch rib cage.

measure three: Keeping arm next to head, shoulders well back, look up, lift chin. Slowly bend to backward arch. Push hips forward, knees firm, head back. Reach hand toward the floor.

measure four: Lift chest up first, head back. Slowly straighten the back, hand coming up last. Bring right arm out to side, stand still.

Repeat four times. The fourth time, release knees, touch hand to the floor in back. Straighten up. Turn around and repeat the entire exercise with left arm moving.

BENT KNEE LIFT

(For older students)

This barre exercise leads directly to many of the dance movements. The emphasis is on the direction of the body and chest curving to "forward in," "side over," and "back lift up." The movement is developed by feeling the full weight of the legs and arms. Become aware of the lifting in resistance to gravity. The pull of the weight of the limbs creates tension and then release.

STARTING POSITION
Left hand on barre, face forward. Stand with heels together, toes out in "V" shape, right arm down at side.

DESCRIPTION
measure one: Relevé to half-toe on left foot. Bring body forward, bend from waist, contract stomach muscles. Lower head to the front. Move right arm

and shoulder forward and up to head at ear level, wrist bent, fingers down (Figure 2.6a). Feel tension of back. Bring right knee up forward to hip height.

measure two: Return to starting position. Release. Stand straight.

measure three: Relevé to half-toe on left foot. Bend over at waist to right side. Bring right arm out to side, shoulder level. Bend head to right shoulder. Lift right knee out to side under right arm (Figure 2.6b). Feel tension of side, over right knee.

measure four: Return to starting position. Release. Stand straight.

measure five: Relevé to half-toe on left foot. Lift right arm up overhead, look up. Lift right leg well up in back, knee bent (attitude) (Figure 2.6c). Feel stretch of arch upward.

measure six: Return to starting position. Release. Stand straight.

Turn around and repeat the entire exercise with the left leg.

After all barre exercises:

Step away from the barre. With feet apart, bend forward, massage the small of the back, shake the shoulders, shake the arms and hands. Straighten body. Rotate the head and chin.

2.6 *Bent knee lift.*

3

WALKING

While walking, strive to be aware that the body weight is kept centered. Do not move from side to side, only forward. One foot must step in front of the other. When practicing the walk, keep the head at an even level. Make the transition of the step smoothly. Keep shoulders free from tension. Walk with chest, head, and chin high. Reflect the legato of the music. Work for sureness without strain. After the rhythm is certain, add dramatic images suited to the music; for example, for younger students use story characters or animals; for older students use a variety of personalities or dramatic situations. Encourage imaginative responses.

BASIC WALK
(For all ages)

MUSIC	Schubert's Grande March op. 40, no. 1
TIME	4/4, common time. Walk in slow, moderate, and fast tempos. Learn to step on different accents within the same musical phrase.
STARTING POSITION	Stand in a circle, facing center, with heels together, toes slightly turned out, weight forward. Hold arms loosely down at sides with the elbows turned out. Shake hands and feet to loosen before starting.

FLOOR PATTERN   After the preparation steps, turn to walk clockwise. Leave space between students.

DESCRIPTION   To prepare the step, face the center, shift weight to stand fully on right foot. Lift left knee up in front, just high enough to let toes clear off the floor. Let foot hang down relaxed in front of supporting foot. Stand firm with hips tucked under body (Figure 3.1a). Lower the left foot slowly. Touch toes down gently until entire foot is fully flat on the floor. Shift the weight of the hips forward onto the left foot by pushing the right leg in back until the heel is off the floor. Release heel so that it drops inward (Figure 3.1b). Keep ball of foot in back, on the floor as long as possible. One complete step has now been taken. Repeat the entire action several times with each foot.

Since the movement is secure, turn to move clockwise in the circle. Walk in various tempos, starting with slow. After some practice, change to moderate and then to fast. Stop and listen carefully to the beat of the music for several

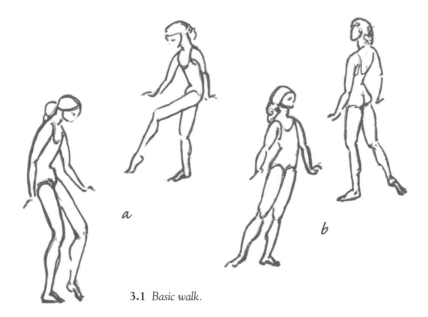

a

b

3.1 *Basic walk.*

measures before starting. Start to walk with a new phrase of music. Establish which beat to follow with clapping and stamping.

Slow

Accent the first beat of each measure. Count aloud, four beats for each step.

and: Lift right knee.

one: Place right foot down slowly.

two: Shift weight forward onto right full foot.

three: Stretch left leg back, heel in.

four: Slowly bring left knee forward in front as described in Basic Walk.

Moderate

Accent the first and third beats. Count aloud, two beats for each step.

and: Lift right knee.

one: Step forward onto right foot, stretch left leg in back.

two: Hold right leg extended in back.

three: Bring left knee up and step forward onto left foot.

four: Hold right leg extended in back.

Fast

Four steps, count aloud, one on each beat of the measure. Walk as described in Basic Walk. Step lightly on each beat, put toes down first. Keep weight forward all the time. Stretch the back leg on each step.

PATTERNS FOR CLASSWORK

WALK WITH GESTURES
Greeting, Leading and Parting

(For mixed ages, all levels)

This pattern gives the student an opportunity to make the walk step part of a dramatic interchange of gestures and body lines. At the same time it demands rhythmic security. The result is a dual awareness, which, in this dance experience, is very important.

MUSIC	Schubert's "Rosamond," Entr'acte no. 2
TIME	2/4, moderate, two beats for each step. The music continues until all have returned to their places.
STARTING POSITION	The class stands in two single files at the sides of the dance space, along opposite walls. All face to the rear, except the first couple. The floor pattern will emerge during the walk. At the end of the exercise, all will have changed places once and then returned to their original places.
FLOOR PATTERN	Walk to the center rear to meet partner. Walk forward with partner. Partner at left passes in front. Separate and walk to new line.
DESCRIPTION	The students at the rear end of each line face each other. Raise right hand to chest with elbow up and out, bend wrist outward, point fingers in to chest (Figure 3.2a). Step toward partner, walk on every second beat of the music as described in Moderate Walk, two beats for each step. As partners approach, extend right hand with a friendly gesture, palm up, fingers forward (Figure 3.2b). Look at each other. When fingers touch, take hands (Figure 3.2c). Both partners turn to face the front. Partner on the right side keeps right elbow forward, arm at chest level. This is the "lead" or "guiding" position. Move the left arm up in back of shoulders of the partner, in a protective gesture, not touching. It remains there

greeting

guiding

parting

a

b

c

d

3.2 *Walking with gestures.*

while both step together with heads tilting toward each other. Advance, step together. Keep eye contact.

When the front of the space is reached, the lead figure pauses to move the partner around in front and over to the right. Raise both right arms high, still holding hands. Partner on the right now faces to the rear. Release hands slowly, reluctantly. Bodies form an arc with both right hands high. Left arms are out at shoulder level. Bend heads toward each other (Figure 3.2d). Continue to walk away toward the side. Make one gesture of farewell, keeping the hands high as the distance increases. Give a final glance when the opposite lines are reached. First pair is now last.

Everyone in both lines moves down and new partners start. Each new couple starts when the previous couple parts. Everyone in both lines has a chance to lead. The leader is always on the right side, leading with right elbow and arm. Both step out on the right foot to keep in step throughout. Everyone returns to original lines, with the second partner leading.

Procession

(For mixed ages)

This walk strives for legato in gestures and movements. Feel changes with the dynamics of the music and the change from loud to soft. Match large steps with large gestures. Respond without making abrupt breaks. It should have the dignity of a Panathenaic Procession (see Glossary).

MUSIC	Schubert, March op. 40, no. 1; Bach chorales; Beethoven, allegretto movement from Symphony No. 7.
TIME	4/4, lento, maestoso. One step each measure, four beats for each step, as in Basic Walk: Slow.
STARTING POSITION	Stand in a loose group at far corner. Face opposite diagonal corner.
FLOOR PATTERN	Walk in cornered figure-eight: walk to opposite corner, turn to walk across front of space, turn to walk to opposite diagonal corner, turn to walk across rear of space.
DESCRIPTION	Start from rear corner. Walk slowly to opposite corner with firm long steps. As the steps move across the floor, slowly start to raise arms. Lift hands forward, palms up, fingers curved out, elbows bent and curved slightly outward (Figure

3.3 *Procession (walking).*

3.3a). Bring arms up higher and higher while walking toward the corner. Imagine a light weight in each hand; think of carrying a precious gift. Lift chest up and arms forward, look high up to the light. Keep eyes and chin in focus (Figure 3.3b). Drop head back at the corner. Bring hands and head down. Turn to walk across front of space. Step around slowly in the corner to the new direction. Start to lift arms again. Proceed to opposite corner. The arms and head come up at each corner and then come down slowly to change direction. Return to starting place. Finish with arms high, chest lifted (Figure 3.3c).

The pattern can also be done by one dancer at a time, starting from the corner, following the floor pattern in a figure-eight. Watch the space at intersection crossing.

Finish

Start

3.4 *Stride—serpentine pattern.*

The Stride with Calling Gesture

(For intermediate ages, eight to ten years and over)

The Stride is a long, springing step that uses large, heroic gestures to express feelings of comradeship and freedom. This pattern helps in coordinating changes of directions, and asserts the individual in a group pattern.

MUSIC	Schubert, March op. 51, no. 3
TIME	4/4, marcato, moderato. Four steps to each measure, one beat for each step.
STARTING POSITION	Stand in a circle, counterclockwise. After the circle, move to wait in front corner of dance area.
FLOOR PATTERN	Change into a "serpentine" (see Figure 3.4, and Glossary), starting from front corner. Keep winding back. After four direction changes, arrive at rear corner wall.
DESCRIPTION	To begin: step with long steps in circle, lift the knees. Relevé to half-toe on each springing step. Spring up without leaving the floor. Swing the arms in opposition to the feet, keep the chest high.

After the lifted spring step is secure, move out of the circle, change to "serpentine." The gesture with the stride across will be a call or a wave to part, taken to show a new direction. Start with a step out to the right side from front corner. Torso front, look back over left shoulder. Lift left arm to the back, over the head, palm forward (Figure 3.4). Make one high calling gesture with wrist bent in direction of walk. Move hand in direction of walk to point to that direction. Keep the walk sprightly, move arm only one arc in the direction of the steps. Change direction at the wall. Turn toward the rear. Lift right arm to the back, make gesture up and over the head while walking toward the left side.

Continue to change direction for four serpentine patterns until the rear space is reached.

Turning About

(For younger students)

This pattern of walking helps younger students to learn changes of direction and to become aware of phrasing and frontality, to experience design and connections with others, in a pattern of greeting, turning, and parting.

MUSIC   Schubert's "Rosamond," Entr'acte no. 2, andante

TIME   2/4, moderate. Two steps to each measure, one beat for each step.

STARTING POSITION   Two lines standing at the far walls, facing each other. Stand with feet together. Alternate students start from both lines to designated partner.

DESCRIPTION   Every other student extends right arm forward to partner. Walk eight steps lightly. Meet partner midway. Touch fingers, take right hands, lift arms into "loop" position. One partner faces front, one faces rear. Bend elbows at shoulder level, touch corner sides of elbows. Bend wrists, turn fingers in to create a "loop." Hold fingers lightly (Figure 3.5a). Walk around each other clockwise, to the right, eight light steps. The appearance will suggest clockwork figurines. Listen for the musical

3.5 *Turnabout walking pattern.*

phrase without counting aloud. Release hands after completing turnabout. Both partners turn to face front. Bring both arms over far shoulder. Walk back to starting places, looking back over shoulder (Figure 3.5b). Continue until all couples have done the same pattern to the right.

Repeat entire sequence to the left.

It is not necessary to count aloud. Let the students sense the beat of the phrase by listening for the beginning of a new phrase, when each segment of the pattern starts as a new design.

RUNNING AND LEAPING

4

LIGHT TROTTING (SPRINGING) RUN

(For all ages)

The Light Trotting Run introduces the basic playful quality of the springing run. The running step becomes a game with gravity. The harder the push away from the earth, the higher the spring. Each action has an equal and opposite reaction.

MUSIC	Schubert, March op. 40, no. 4
TIME	4/4, moderate, staccato; four springing running steps each measure, one beat for each step.
STARTING POSITION	Stand with heels together. Arms raised out to shoulder level. Elbows rounded, palms facing out and up. Before beginning the run, rise up to half-toe and down on both feet several times, then jump lightly in place. Pay attention to proper breathing with the mouth closed.
FLOOR PATTERN	Large clockwise circle.
DESCRIPTION	Walk with a light spring from the ankles. Move the weight of the body well forward into a tilt. Gradually increase the tempo of the music. As it becomes faster start to push off the

floor with a spring from the back foot to the front foot. Push up hard and land softly. There will now be a light continuous run that resembles a pony-trotting step. Bounce lightly from half-toe to half-toe. Keep heels off the floor. Extend the space between each step. Spring upward more than forward. The spring should be from the ankle up into the knee. Lift knees sharply both in front and in back. Point toes. Keep the weight of the body high, with chest lifted. Work for lightness. Listen for quiet landings. Feel the musical pulse.

PATTERNS FOR CLASSWORK

Serpentine

(For older students, ages ten and older)

The serpentine pattern suggests a meandering brook or the passage of a playful breeze. The student's imagination creates the action of the body and the gestures. The dance is both the object as well as the observer. The floor pattern creates the scene. Feel the rush of air against the body. Move with gestures to the earth and the sky. Suggest the wind bending growing things as it passes. The image of a meandering stream involves ensemble play where each dancer is part of a larger scene.

MUSIC	Schubert-Liszt song, "Wohin"
TIME	4/4, staccato, light accents. Four steps to each measure, one beat for each step.
STARTING POSITION	Stand poised on half-toe, feet together. Single line along left side wall.
FLOOR PATTERN	A serpentine from the rear corner wall to the front. Move forward with each change of direction. Five changes of direction should complete the pattern. Run one behind the other in a single line, follow until final bend at the far wall.
DESCRIPTION	When the music starts, the first person turns to

the front. All follow in the same way, from the starting corner, in single file. Spring run to the right along the rear wall, starting on right foot. Left arm raised high toward the back, right arm low in front. Look back at left hand (Figure 4.1a).

Move left arm gradually down toward the floor (Figure 4.1). Bend body down to look down past the hand at the ground (Figure 4.1c). Keep the running step moving to the right while the left arm begins to lift up into the same direction as the run. Lift chest up high, look up at hand (Figure 4.1d). Arrive at the far wall with left hand forward, palm down. At the wall, each change direction, in turn, by turning sharply toward the front. Bring right arm high up in back to start. Run to the left side. Move right arm slowly, bend down low, turn palm forward. Move right arm across and stretch up while running from one side of the room to the other. Again change direction. Run to the right with the left arm gesture down and up. Change again at the far wall. Run to the left side with right arm gesture down and up. The last crossing will be to the right with left arm gesture down and up. There will be four changes of direction to complete five crossings. Finish with a reach up and a deep breath.

To understand the gestures more clearly: before starting out, while standing ready, review the mime of the arms. Look and bend down as if to touch, then lift the hands and look up. Stand with feet wide apart.

4.1 *Serpentine—light trot run.*

Weaving with Partners

(For mixed levels and ages)

This appears as a game for two. A friendly challenge. One partner holds back as the other darts forward. Faces turn to each other. The partner on the outer rim of the circle holds back a little so that the inner partner can surge ahead and change places without stopping. Each partner adjusts quickly to holding back and surging forward.

MUSIC	Schubert–Liszt song, "The Trout"; Schubert's March op. 21, no. 1, Trio.
TIME	2/2, staccato, with light accent every eight beats.
STARTING POSITION	Hold right hands as described in "Walk with Gestures": Leading, above.
FLOOR PATTERN	See "weaving" in the Glossary; Figure 11.
DESCRIPTION	Run counterclockwise. Partners change places at each corner of space. The space is angled three times, three successive corners after the start.
	Run lightly as in light trotting (springing) run. Start together, hold right hands lightly. Be a comfortable distance apart. Run four measures, eight light steps. Keep arms up. Look at each other. Release hands. Inside partner starts to pass forward to the right, taking accent and large steps in front of outside partner; outside partner takes smaller steps. Eight runs to crossover at the first corner. Both partners run eight steps together. The person on the inner rim now surges forward with eight larger steps to cross in front and become the outside partner at the second corner. Inside person changes again after eight run steps together, takes accent and larger steps to run ahead and be the outside partner. The inside partner always surges forward and past the outside partner. Keep eye contact throughout. Bend down low to pass close under the lifted arms. Lift chest and head on the accent to pass. The outside partner adjusts with smaller steps and moves to

the left to become the inside partner. Each has a turn to move ahead and then hold back. Take eight steps together, then eight steps to change.

Note: This weaving pattern can also be done with the Skip and the Swing Skip (see Chapter 5).

FAST, LIGHT RUN

This run, which gives the illusion of great speed and lightness, actually takes the body over large spaces in the least time. To perform it properly requires agility, breath control, and surefootedness.

MUSIC   Schubert impromptus or Chopin etudes

TIME   The music must flow continuously, without break. Breathe with the musical phrase.

STARTING POSITION   Stand high up on tiptoes. Reach hands high overhead, look up. Drop forward into a deep lunge with front knee well bent. Stretch chin forward. Stretch both arms out in back. Hold this position and check for alignment; feel forward thrust. Return to first image, hands high up. Repeat lunge. Do this several times, toward the corner, before starting from high position.

FLOOR PATTERN   The complete action covers a figure-eight floor pattern with one running spurt in each direction.

DESCRIPTION   Start from corner, reach up (Figure 4.2a). Lunge. Do not stay in this position but run forward in a spurt of small steps toward the opposite corner. Keep body well bent forward, with chin and eyes in focus to the forward corner (Figure 4.2b). Gradually lift chest upward. Then the arms. Run on half-toe forward to opposite corner, lift face up. Look high up overhead (Figure 4.2c). Lift arms from the back; be certain to raise arms out to the side, then upward (Figure 4.2d). Reach up with head back, take a deep breath. Pause (Figure 4.2e).

Make a half turn into new direction, across the

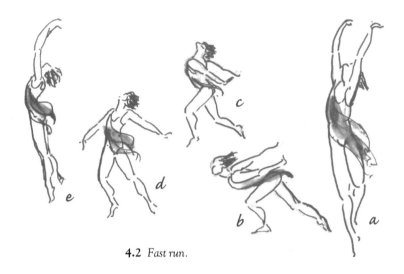

4.2 *Fast run.*

front of the space. Lower arms, first out to the side, then to the back. Bring chest forward, again reach arms up. Run in sequence as before, to the diagonal corner. Pause, change directions. Repeat run sequence across rear of the space.

When done in small groups, wait at each corner until everyone has arrived. Keep the same spatial relationships constantly. All move together to the next corner. The effect is that of a flock of birds moving as one. The response to the music will be in long breath phrases, rather than in specific rhythmic beat.

LONG RUN ("AMAZON")

(For older and more advanced students)

This running step helps in the imagery of strength. It is based on figures in Greek art representing the power of the militant Amazon. In class work it helps to create group awareness. The Long Run requires muscular tension and elevation. It also extends endurance.

MUSIC   Schubert, March op. 27, no. 2

TIME   4/4, marcato, moderate tempo, strong accents; four steps each measure, one beat for each step.

FLOOR PATTERN   Circle around the space, then diagonal, then figure-eight.

DESCRIPTION   Walk around the room with long steps as in Walk with Gestures: The Stride. Swing arms in opposition to feet. Clench fists, raise elbows high. Chest up, weight forward. Change the tempo, become gradually slower. Push the weight off the floor. Spring into a long, high-stepping run. Swing the arms high. Mark the accents of the music to give time for greater elevation, for each thrust up and forward. Lift the knees high front and rear. Land lightly on toes.

For practice, change floor pattern to diagonal from rear to front opposite corner. When the step is strong, change to figure-eight. Begin in the far rear corner. Move on diagonal with eight long run steps. Start with left foot and right hand, fist clenched. Turn at corner, take eight long run steps across front. Turn at corner, take eight long run steps on diagonal. Turn at corner, take eight long run steps across rear.

PARTNERS

Start shoulder to shoulder, both with right hand, left foot. Take eight long steps diagonally to corner. Turn at corner, stay one behind the other. Take eight long steps across the front. Turn at corner, move shoulder to shoulder, face corner diagonal. Take eight long steps diagonally to opposite corner. Turn at corner, one behind the other, single file. Take eight long steps across rear.

PHALANX:
Repeat design with three dancers, shoulder to shoulder. Repeat design, double the line for six dancers.

PHALANX:
Start in two lines of three (six dancers), one behind the other. All start with left foot and right hand, shoulder to shoulder. Run eight leaps to opposite corner, turn sharply. Run eight leaps, double file, keep together, across front, turn sharply. Run eight leaps, turn sharply, all to diagonal corner, shoulder to shoulder, double line. Run eight leaps, turn sharply, double line, across rear.

Make sure that the lead student at the corners moves fast enough to maintain the lead.

LEAP, RUN, RUN

(For intermediate levels)

This is a combination of the leap and the run, used in much of Duncan's choreography. In class, it concentrates on elevation, strength, and endurance.

MUSIC	Schubert, "Marche Militaire," op. 51, no. 3, Trio
TIME	2/4, moderate, marcato. Four beats for each measure. Strong accent on first beat of every measure.
STARTING POSITION	Stand with weight on left leg, mark accent with right foot by light stamping beat. After beating four measures proceed to leap in a circle.
FLOOR PATTERN	Counterclockwise circle.
DESCRIPTION	Leap on first accent of each measure. Stand on the left foot with right knee up in front.

and: Spring up and over from left foot.

one: Land lightly on right foot. Extend left foot in back.

and two: Walk two steps, right foot, left foot.

and: Pause.

Continue with left knee and foot up and over. Two steps, left foot, right foot. Pause.

Continue counterclockwise around the room. Regulate the tempo of the music. Turn the walk step into a run step. Pause to wait for accent beat on "and" to leap over each time. Leap with alternate feet each time. Keep arms out at shoulder level. Alternate; right leap two runs, then left leap two runs.

PATTERN FOR CLASSWORK

Partners

MUSIC AND TIME	Same as Leap, Run, Run.
STARTING POSITION	All stand in single file at far side walls. Face rear. First partners face each other, raise arms out. Listen to the first accented beat of the music; tap the right foot four times for four measures.
DESCRIPTION	*measures one–four:* Take four leap and run combinations to meet at center rear. Start with right foot forward, arms out to side. Lift head and chest on each high leap. Lift the knee bent in front, extended way high in back.
	measures 4–8: Take four leap, run, run combinations forward, together with partner. Compete for height, look at each other.
	measures 9–12: Separate to right and left. Take four leap, run, run combinations. Alternate left, right. Return to starting positions.
	measures 13–16: Next partners: four stamps with right foot, and continue the pattern until all have had a turn. Practice with scarves held overhead.

FAST RUN WITH HIGH LEAP

(For all levels and ages)

This movement is the culmination of all the foregoing. To run the fastest and lightest, to leap the highest. The run must be surefooted and the leap up dramatic as well as high. The dance statement is completely free but under absolute control. An explosion of strength and lightness going up but a sureness of the landing, acknowledging gravity with a firm, ankle spring up and a secure but soft knee to land and run forward.

MUSIC	Mendelssohn, scherzo from "Midsummer Night's Dream"; or Chopin etudes
TIME	Constant rushing tempo. Listen for phrasing to begin.
STARTING POSITION	Place a long jump rope on the floor midway down the room, on a diagonal angle across space. All assemble in far corner of space. Stand in single file against the side wall, face rear. All wait for single turn. The person whose turn it is faces the opposite corner.
FLOOR PATTERN	From corner to corner. Diagonal from rear to opposite corner.
DESCRIPTION	Bend forward as in preparing the Fast, Light Run (see Figure 4.2). Run as in Fast, Light Run until about two feet in front of the rope. Push back foot and spring forward and up off the floor. Lift right knee well up in front. Raise left leg as high as possible in the back. Arch back, lift arms up

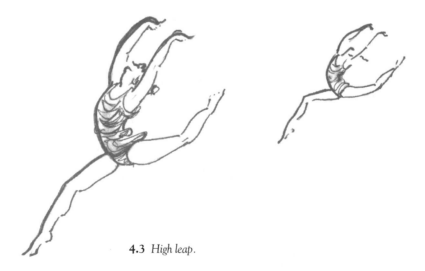

4.3 *High leap.*

overhead, look up. Sustain (Figure 4.3). Land on the right foot lightly with a soft knee, toes first. Bend right knee to receive the weight of landing. Lift the weight up quickly and run lightly back to the corner with arms raised and head high.

The rope is gradually raised as the students progress. The rope can be held lightly by two students or controlled at one end by the teacher. Hold the rope loosely to let go if the students' knees are not lifted high enough to leap over. The line starts with the shorter children making lower leaps. Lift the rope a little higher for each student. Students should be encouraged to work for an elevation that equals their own shoulder height. Make sure the run is forward and low on the half-toe and that the leap lands on the toes lightly with a soft knee, and then the run continues forward to the corner.

The competition is for individual progress rather than class place, although the place in line may change from class to class.

5

SKIPPING

The dancing skip is based on the normal action and natural movement of the simple skip. In the Duncan dance vocabulary, it becomes an encounter with space—a passage that connects with earth beneath and air above as it responds to the dynamics of the music. It can range from delicate staccato to bounding push.

HIGH SKIP

MUSIC	Schubert, March op. 121, no. 1
TIME	6/8, staccato, syncopated: "and–one, and–two, etc." Two skips each measure, three beats for each skip.
STARTING POSITION	Stand in a line at far corner, awaiting turn. Stand high on half-toe, raise arms out to shoulder height, elbows rounded out.
FLOOR PATTERN	Counterclockwise circle, once around the room, at first each person singly. When all have had a turn, all follow behind the leader (all should have a chance to lead in time).
DESCRIPTION	The skip is done high on the half-toe, the lifted knee is raised sharply up in front, the bent leg forming a right angle during the strong spring up. Keep the supporting knee

firm and point the toes as the foot leaves the floor (Figure 5.1a).

When dancing the skip, follow the melodic line with the arms and hands, while the skip goes sharply upward and forward. Imagine companions. Create gestures of friendship. Move the hands to relate to sky and earth. Respond to the dynamic changes in the music with higher skips for loud music (forte) and smaller skips for soft music (pianissimo).

PATTERN FOR CLASSWORK

Partners

(For ages five to eight)

For practice, use play dances like "Skip to My Lou." One child in the center skips around and chooses a partner. Take the partner's right hand high up. Skip in place around each other. High Skip throughout. Partners look at each other. One partner returns to place in the circle; the other chooses a new partner. Other skipping dance games can be made with "Shoo Fly" or "Turkey in the Straw."

LONG SKIP ("AMAZON")

The Long Skip has the characteristic of strength and the challenge of elevation. The chest is always high and forward, the facial expression is determined. This skip, although high, should descend quietly. Work for legato transitions. Also, practice alternating one skip high and more accented with one small skip. This will help the person to sense an awareness of energy release.

MUSIC   Schubert, March op. 121, no. 1

TIME   4/4, marcato, syncopated: "and–one, and–two." Two skips each measure, two syncopated beats for each skip.

5.1 *Skipping.*

STARTING POSITION	Stand in far rear corner. Face diagonal corner. Stagger the start after eight skips. Stamp or clap while awaiting turn.
FLOOR PATTERN	Skip forward from one corner to opposite corner. Wait in line at the opposite far wall. After some practice for long, strong movements, use patterns for classwork.
DESCRIPTION	Lift knee forward, foot in front. Swing arms, with fists clenched, in opposition to legs, right hand to left knee, alternating. Swing arms deeply, elbows bent forward. Push the weight of the body upward and forward (Figure 5.1b). Prepare the pointed toes in front to land lightly and push off as soon as the floor is touched. Create a long, high action. Be sure to spring up high off the floor.

PATTERNS FOR CLASSWORK

Figure-Eight for One

MUSIC AND TIME	Same as Long Skip ("Amazon").
STARTING POSITION	Right foot and left hand forward.
DESCRIPTION	Step on right foot. Skip up with left knee and right hand. Eight skips forward on diagonal from rear corner to front corner. Turn sharply. Eight skips straight across front of dance space. Turn sharply. Eight skips on diagonal to opposite corner. Turn sharply. Eight skips straight across rear of dance space.

Figure-Eight for Two

MUSIC AND TIME	Same as Long Skip ("Amazon").
STARTING POSITION	Stand shoulder to shoulder, face diagonal corner.
DESCRIPTION	Eight skips side by side, forward on diagonal from rear to front corner. Turn sharply. Eight skips one

behind the other, across front. Turn sharply. Eight skips side by side, on diagonal to opposite corner. Turn sharply. Eight skips, one behind the other, across rear.

Figure-Eight for Three

MUSIC AND TIME	Same as Long Skip ("Amazon").
STARTING POSITION	Stand shoulder to shoulder; face diagonal corner.
DESCRIPTION	Follow pattern for two. The leader must be alert to retain place. The center dancer is the anchor position.

ROUND SKIP

The Round Skip helps to achieve smooth weight changes. Use this skip in combination with waltz steps for creative improvisation.

MUSIC	Schubert waltzes
TIME	3/4, waltz; one skip to each measure, "one–two–three" for each skip.
STARTING POSITION	All stand at the rear wall, facing front, high on half-toe.
FLOOR PATTERN	Move straight forward to the front of the work space.
DESCRIPTION	*and:* Step forward on right foot.
	one: Raise left knee out to side, foot pointed out and down.
	two–three: Move entire left leg around and over across right leg. Hop up on the right leg (Figure 5.1c).
	and–one: Bring left foot down.
	two–three: Hop on right foot.
	Continue alternating round skip. Keep arms stretched out to the sides.

SWING SKIP OR HOP SKIP

This dance movement is very important for coordination and self-confidence. Work for smoothness and strength. Move the body from the center, curving in on the skip up, chest up and arching back on the hop forward.

MUSIC   Schubert's March op. 121, no. 2, Back Gigues

TIME   6/8; one Swing Skip each measure, six beats for each Swing Skip: up three beats, forward three beats.

STARTING POSITION   Stand on half-toe, arms out to side, shoulder height, at side of dance space. Starting from corner, move singly at first, then two-by-two, then in a group all together.

FLOOR PATTERN   Counterclockwise circle, singly or in groups.

DESCRIPTION   *and–one:* Skip up with right knee high (Figure 5.2a).

two–three: Put right foot down, hop, swinging left leg to back, knee turned out and lifted high (Figure 5.2b).

four: Bring left leg forward with a spring up. Left knee is forward, with foot in front pointed.

five–six: Hop up in the air, body and chest high.

Continue, left foot going down and right foot

5.2 *Swing skip or hop skip.*

swinging back, hop on left foot. Continue,
alternating sides. The action becomes a continuous skip up and hop forward.

Add the arm movement for the hop when
coordination of the legs is established: step
forward on right foot, look back over left shoulder
and swing and lift both arms over to the right.
Bend body, curve back.

PATTERN FOR CLASSWORK

Partners

All the high skipping and swing skipping can also be done in the
same leading pattern suggested for Walk with Gestures or Weaving, as
described in Light Trotting Run, changing places at the corners
(Figure 5.3; see also Glossary and Figure G.1).

5.3 *Leading partners.*

6

THE WALTZ

(For intermediate to advanced students)

The waltz is essential to much of the technique and choreography of Duncan Dance movements. The waltz should be smooth, but lightly accented. The weight of the body is carried high. The ankles are elastic, so that one moves with a soft spring. The first accent of each measure is always a lift upward and over that creates a wavelike flow as a distinctive characteristic.

BASIC WALTZ FORWARD

MUSIC	Schubert or Johann Strauss waltzes
TIME	3/4, slow to moderate, strong accents; three steps to one measure, one beat for each movement.
STARTING POSITION	Face front, feet together, hands at sides.
FLOOR PATTERN	In a line side by side, move forward.
DESCRIPTION	*and:* Stand very high on balls of both feet.
	one: Step over: lift right foot, step forward onto the extended toe, lifting weight up, over, and down to full right foot.
	two: Slowly draw left foot instep to touch right heel.

55

three: Rise up high on balls of both feet. Right toe leading in front, take a very small step up and forward with right foot.

Repeat all three counts, starting with left foot.

Continue to move forward, waltzing with alternate feet: left—two three, right—two three. Always lift high up and over on the first accent of each measure.

After the step is mastered, practice the waltz holding hands lightly at shoulder height (Figure 6.1). All in a line move forward together. When the line reaches the front, separate, run lightly to the rear to start again.

BALANCÉ (ROCKING) WALTZ WITH FORWARD AND BACKWARD WALTZ COMBINATION

This dance pattern helps to attain freedom of movement with an expressed awareness of space. It also demands accountability of gesture—to companions, to the earth, to the free air above!

TIME	3/4; complete pattern consists of eight measures: six rocking waltz steps (forward and backward) for six measures, followed by two forward waltz steps for two measures.
STARTING POSITION	Stand as in Basic Waltz, arms out at shoulder height.
FLOOR PATTERN	Singly or in small groups. Move to front of space (see Time, above).
DESCRIPTION	*measure one:* Waltz forward on right foot, as described in Basic Waltz. Swing arms up and forward at the sides. Look to the right. Bend forward slightly.
	measure two: Waltz backward on left foot—*one:* step back on left foot, up and over; *two:* draw right heel back to left foot instep, feet together, stand down; *three:* rise up on both toes, step in place with left foot up and down. Swing arms down and back. Look to the left, lift the chest (Figure 6.1).

6.1 *Waltzing.*

measure three: Waltz step forward on right foot. Swing arms up and forward. Look right.

measure four: Waltz step backward on left foot. Swing arms down and back. Look left.

measure five: Waltz step forward on right foot. Swing arms up and forward. Look right.

measure six: Waltz step backward on left foot. Swing arms down and back. Look left.

measures seven–eight: Waltz step forward on right foot; cross arms down in front and look down. Waltz step forward on left foot; lift and uncross arms, look up, lift chest.

RUNNING WALTZ

The Running Waltz should help the person achieve a spirited, light, continuous flow of accented action. The body moves from side to side with the arms and chest. The feet carry the body well forward. The body bends to the direction of the arm movement. Focus the eyes in the direction of the gesture, which reaches out each time.

TIME	3/4; one measure to complete the pattern.
STARTING POSITION	Stand in a circle, face clockwise, feet together, arms out at shoulder height.
DESCRIPTION	Move rapidly through the space. The first step is

a small leap on "and–one." Complete the waltz step on "two–three."

and–one: Rise high on balls of feet, spring forward with long run step on right foot.

two: Draw left foot up to right foot on half-toe. Keep knees relaxed, ankles springy.

three: Take a small running step forward on right foot.

Continue with long run on left foot, draw up right foot, small running steps on left foot.

Arm movement to synchronize (practice separately):

one: On forward spring to right foot look to the right, move right hand with gesture from center chest out to far right side.

two–three: Hold gesture, look far out, until end of the measure. For left side, use left arm.

The Running Waltz can be practiced in Serpentine or Figure-Eight patterns.

HALF-TURN WALTZ

The Half-Turn Waltz is intended to help the dancer experience and observe the turn, either to the right or to the left, and to enjoy the *volte* of the waltz in turning and the exhilaration of turning in a continuous direction, a half-turn at a time.

TIME	3/4; two measures to complete the pattern.
STARTING POSITION	Stand in a circle, face clockwise, feet together. Hold right hand high overhead, wrist relaxed, palm down. Place left hand on hip, fingers to the back.

WALTZ WITH GESTURE

DESCRIPTION	*measure one:* Waltz step forward on right foot, bring hand and arm forward. Look toward right hand palm up.

measure two: Half turn around to the right: waltz step backward on left foot in clockwise direction. Lift right arm up, look over left shoulder.

measure three: Half turn around to the right: waltz step forward on right foot. Gesture forward with right hand.

measure four: Repeat actions of measures two and three, continue half turns to the right.

After practice to the right, change direction and begin the entire movement, starting with Basic Waltz steps forward on the left foot, move left arm forward. Move in counterclockwise direction, making half turns to the left.

ARMS AND HANDS TO SYNCHRONIZE
(PRACTICE SEPARATELY.)

measure one: Right hand to chest, fingers in toward body, elbow lifted at the same height as the hand. Gesture with right hand straight forward, hand moves from chest to person in front. Open hand, palm up, stretch fingers.

measure two: Bring right arm back and up. Raise hand high overhead, wrist dropped, fingers held loosely.

Repeat.

Continue to make the gesture, first forward, then overhead. Practice with left hand, dancers facing counterclockwise.

WALTZ LIFT AND TWIRL

(For more advanced students)

STARTING
POSITION
Stand at the side wall. Face to the front. The right shoulder is forward to lead across the dance space to the right, the right arm is across the chest. Look down (Figure 6.2a). Stand with weight back on left foot. Right knee is relaxed.

For class work, stand in a line, one dancer behind the other.

Exercise One: Arms for Waltz Lift

TIME 3/4; two measures to complete the pattern.

DESCRIPTION *and–one:* Look up high, lift the chest, at the same time step on right foot out to the right.

two: Swing right hand up high over the head, palm out. Hold.

three: Bring left arm back out to the left, shoulder height. All movements connect quickly.

four: Step back on left foot, bring weight down.

five: Bring right arm back down across the chest.

six: Look down, relax right knee and foot. Lower the chest. Round the back.

Practice for eight measures, four lifts up: one measure to lift; one measure to bring weight down.

Exercise Two: Lift Up and Waltz Back

TIME 3/4; two measures to complete the pattern.

DESCRIPTION *measure one:* Lift up to the right—*one:* step out to right side, hop up on right foot; *two:* look up, swing right arm up, hand is up, lift chest, left arm in back to shoulder height; *three:* raise left leg up in back with bent knee turned out. Sustain the hop lightly (see Figure 6.2b).

measure two: four–five–six: Lower left foot. Waltz step back on left foot with full weight. Bring right arm down across the chest, look down, bend over slightly and lower the left arm in back. Bring both arms across the waist (see Figure 6.2a).

Practice to expand out on hop, and to close in on the backward waltz.

6.2 *Waltz—lift up and draw back.*

Exercise Three: Complete Lift, Waltz Twirl

TIME   3/4; two measures to complete the pattern.

DESCRIPTION   *one:* Step forward on right foot, lift body up with the hop, swing right arm up with palm out. Lift left arm back. Move to connect all movements quickly.

two: Lift left leg in back, knee bent and turned out.

three: Sustain lift with arched back, arm up.

four–five–six: Return left foot to floor, to step around in forward direction. Twirl right completely around in place with one triplet waltz step. Keep feet close together. Look quickly over the right shoulder, focus again into direction, bring hands down lightly across chest. Pause.

Continue to move forward with the lift on the right foot. It is advisable to start slowly with the first two preparatory exercises, until coordination is established for this exercise.

To allow more opportunity for speedier movements, start the "twirl" turn from the corner of the dance space and move diagonally to the opposite corner. Four Lift, Waltz Twirls take eight measures. Hold the last turn with both arms held high, take a deep breath. Finish facing front.

Exercise Four: The Spin Twirl

To advance the technique, here is a variation for greater speed.

TIME	3/4; one measure to complete the pattern.
DESCRIPTION	Lift, spring up, then spin around quickly. Start again on the first accent. Lift the arm up into the direction of the turn, circle the hand on the hop, high up. Practice at first slowly, then gradually increase the tempo.

Exercise Five: Pattern Combination

TIME	3/4; eight measures to complete the pattern.
DESCRIPTION	Combine the slower Waltz Twirls with the faster Spin Twirls. Two Waltz Twirls and three Spin Twirls complete eight measures. In the last measure, finish with both arms high. This pattern is a good aerobic dance to increase endurance and breath control.

FLYING DART LIFT AND WALTZ

This dance step is airborne. Sustain the body with deep breathing and long gestures. Look to the companion, move with large gestures. Then imagine others—indicate unseen multitudes! Feel the energy move from body center out to space.

TIME	3/4; two measures to complete the pattern.
STARTING POSITION	Stand in a circle facing clockwise, feet together. Hands crossed over the chest. Look down.
DESCRIPTION	*and–one*: Step out to the right, hop up on right foot. Lift and swing right hand and arm in to circle, left arm out. Look past hand.

two: Lift left leg high in back, arch back and look to center.

three: Sustain lift in the air.

four: Bring left leg down. Step forward on the left foot, move clockwise in a circle.

five: Step forward on right foot, bring arms back down across chest.

six: Step forward on left foot. Lift up on left foot with right leg up high in back. Arch back, look out to space, chest high.

Continue to lift, step, and step, alternating feet. Travel clockwise in the circle. The movement should be like flying. Both arms move out from one side to the other.

VARIATION

Partners, with Lift on Beat Four

TIME 3/4; four measures to complete the pattern in and out.

STARTING POSITION Form two lines at opposite far walls; face the rear. First pair moves away from line and faces front to dance out into the spaces. Stagger start every four measures.

DESCRIPTION *one–two:* Step with inside foot toward partner, both arms out, shoulder level.

three: Take second step, bring feet together. Bring inside hand to chest.

four: Step hop, fly up on inside foot, raise inside arm high. Lift outside foot high in back, arch the chest.

five–six: Hold in the air (Figure 6.3).

one–two–three: Step away from partner and move toward the front of the dance space.

four–five–six: The flying gesture. Lift the face, focus the eyes. Hold in the air.

Move from side to side. Progress forward until the front, then separate. Return to line.

6.3 *Flying dart lift and waltz.*

7

SWAYING

The movements of swaying are among the most characteristic and unique of all the genuine qualities of Duncan Dance. Inspired by a fragmented armless classical Greek statue called "Maenad," Isadora found the primary movement she thought was so pure and universal that it should not be classified as only "Greek." Here was the very image of that source of movement through the upper torso—from the center, the solar plexus—that ebbs and flows in ongoing renewal. In nature itself it can be seen in the movements of the trees against the wind, yielding and resisting. Transfer a similar imaginative reaction into the body and it becomes, in turn, passive and active—the two important responses of her New Dance.

BASIC SWAY: TORSO ONLY

MUSIC   Chopin preludes, such as op. 28, no. 8.

TIME   2/4, adagio tempo, legato action; two measures for each change of weight.

STARTING POSITION   Stand with weight fully on left foot, right foot relaxed, feet slightly apart. Arms down at sides. Head bent down to the left.

DESCRIPTION   Active: *measures one–two:* take a small step on right foot to the right side, shift weight over to

65

right foot slowly, lift chest up and over to the right.

Passive: *measures three–four:* release head to go up and around after the chest lift, look up, then look down from left to right. Upper chest is dropped over right foot.

Repeat to the left side, reversing direction.

Continue swaying in place. The movement of the chest follows a figure-eight. It helps to keep fingertips lightly touching the chest, to follow the flow of the action.

SWAY WITH ARMS OVERHEAD

MUSIC AND TIME
Same as Basic Sway.

STARTING POSITION
Stand as before with weight on the right foot. Stretch both arms up, parallel, overhead. Bend body from the upper chest to the right side. Look up at both hands.

DESCRIPTION
Action flows continuously from side to side. Remain in place (Figure 7.1).

7.1 *Sway.*

Press upward: *one:* take a deep breath, lift chin, stretch up from chest. Step to the left with left foot. Rise up to half-toe on both feet; *two:* press the left side of chest up and around to the left, arms overhead. Follow slowly, move after the chest to the left. Move head last, after arms, stretch the left side of the neck.

Descend to bend over to the side: *three:* release the upward push, bring the weight to the center over both feet, high on half-toe, press the whole upper torso around and over to the left side, arms follow after; *four:* move arms, hands, and fingers against the air, press then release to the left, move head over to left shoulder, release to look down to the left. Bring arms over to the left side, bend to the left. Eyes follow the direction of hands, palms of hands press against the air.

Take two measures to sway to each side. Drop the wrists at the end of each direction. The "active" part of the sway occurs from up on the first beat to the second. The "passive" descends from the third to the fourth beats.

SWAY AND LIGHT RUN

(For all ages)

MUSIC	Mendelssohn, "On Wings of Song"
TIME	3/4 legato; four measures to complete pattern.
STARTING POSITION	Stand up high on half-toe on both feet as in Fast, Light Run. Face front. Arms up high overhead. Look up past hands.
FLOOR PATTERN	From rear left side of space, run side to side to front of space.
DESCRIPTION	The running is similar to the Fast, Light Run, but here the run moves to the side. The upper body moves as previously described in Sway with Arms Overhead. To start, bend body over to the left,

then sway to the right. Synchronize the sway to take the full four measures as the run moves to the opposite side of the space. Keep face to the front. At the end of the fourth measure, drop arms over to the right side. The hands will describe an arc, such as the sky, while the feet run lightly over to each side.

Follow the phrase of the music. Move from left to right across and forward each time in a zig-zag pattern.

For continuous action, begin in a circle, moving in and out, then change to zig-zag, facing front.

For improvisation, discuss and describe images such as the actions of the wind, the birds, singing. Encourage variety of floor pattern to include twirling and swooping up and down. Let the actions emerge freely. This dance can be done singly or in small groups that make way for each other as they pass. This experience helps to create awareness of space and the exhilaration of moving freely but responsibly.

8

THE POLKA

The polka is a spirited dance rhythm that offers an opportunity for learning independence as well as group coherence, while at the same time opening up to the full emotional release of the joyous and playful variety of patterns.

BASIC POLKA

(For all ages)

MUSIC	Beethoven, "Ruins of Athens"; Johann Strauss, Polkas; Smetana, Polka from "Schwanda."
TIME	4/4, marcato. Count "and, one, two, three" for each measure of four beats, with full accent on *and*.
STARTING POSITION	Arms out at sides at shoulder height. Stand high, on balls of feet.
FLOOR PATTERN	Counterclockwise circle, singly or in groups.
DESCRIPTION	Skip, run, run.

and: Skip up high with right knee up, raise arms up, lift chest and head with skip (see Skipping).

one: Moving in the circle, small run forward on right foot, half-toe.

two: Small run forward on left foot, half-toe.

three: Step forward on right foot.

Continue to move forward in circle.

and: Skip up high with left knee up, raise arms up, lift chest and head with skip.

one: Small run forward on left foot, half-toe.

two: Small run forward on right foot, half-toe.

three: Step forward on left foot.

To continue, polka right and left, moving in counterclockwise circle. The lifted knee alternates. Throw hands and arms up high and forward lightly on the lift. Bend forward during the small runs, hands and arms down. Control the descent. Eyes look directly forward, as in Basic Run.

PATTERNS FOR CLASSWORK

POLKA WITH HANDKERCHIEF GESTURE

MUSIC AND TIME	Same as Basic Polka.
STARTING POSITION	Stand in a circle, face counterclockwise. Hold or pretend to hold a kerchief in the right hand. Place left hand on hip, stretch right arm out to reach away from the circle center. Stand straight. Point left foot forward in direction of circle.
DESCRIPTION	Move as in Basic Polka, but skip, run, run with smaller steps. Bring the knees up sharply on the first accent of each measure.

Preparatory Exercise: Arms Only

measure one: Bring the right arm from out on the right side to over the head and across the chest to the left. Bend to the left side from the waist. Incline head to the left shoulder. Move right hand toward left hip.

measure two: Bend to the right side, from the waist. Bring the right arm up overhead and over to the right. Incline head to right shoulder. Continue bending left and right with arm gesture. Wave the kerchief for eight gestures, eight measures.

COMPLETE POLKA STEP WITH HANDKERCHIEF GESTURE

measure one: To start, stand with left shoulder in to center. Start polka step with left foot forward. Bend to the left, move right hand in to the center.

measure two: Polka step with right foot forward. Bend to the right side, move right hand out to side away from center.

Continue around in counterclockwise direction.

When coordination is established, let the dance feelings develop a joyous expression of complete rhythmic participation in a happy dance.

After some practice, reverse the direction to circle clockwise. Stand in starting position with left hand out and right foot forward. Move left hand from side in to side out.

POLKA THROUGH THE CENTER

MUSIC AND TIME   Same as Basic Polka.

STARTING
POSITION   This polka is done in counterclockwise direction. Emerge from side of space one by one, in single turn.

DESCRIPTION   Move as in Basic Polka, but with smaller runs. Sharp skip up on the forward foot, each first accent lift high up off the floor. Control both arms to move freely out from the sides at shoulder height (Figure 8.1a). Arms follow the melodic line. Dance with free imagery, improvise gestures.

8.1 *Polka (through the center).*

Feet remain in constant rhythm pattern of Basic Polka—skip, run, run—to complete one circle.

Continue polka to center of rear wall. Without stopping, face front, look down, move arms down across body (Figure 8.1b), look up and uncross arms in a wide circular motion, as if up to the sky. Make a free gesture "to the universe" (Figure 8.1c) (see Basic Arm Movements).

When the front of the space is reached, finish

with gesture out. Continue to polka to the right and dance away from waiting group to opposite wall. Make a farewell gesture (Figure 8.1d), left hand high, look back over shoulder.

When each student has had a single turn, all join together, dance the polka around the room until the music ends. This variation can be used at the end of class. The students leave the room, waving as they dance off, still following in line.

REIGEN (RING) WITH SLIDE POLKA

MUSIC AND TIME   Same as Basic Polka.

STARTING POSITION   For group, polka in a circle, arrive in the center of the space. Without stopping the music, pause to take hands in a Grip Lock (see Glossary), arms shoulder height. Right foot marks time by beating the first accent of the polka four times while standing in place. Start with the right foot, do Slide Polka.

DESCRIPTION   Stand in circle, hold hands. Move sideways.

and: Skip to the right side with right knee up, hop on left foot, put right foot down.

one: Slide left foot up to right foot on half-toe. Bring feet together.

two: Small step to the right side with right foot.

three: Lift left knee up, hop on right foot. Step left foot across right foot.

Continue in circling direction, arms held at shoulder height. Make a strong marked accent, so that everyone dances together: come up on "and," the upbeat; go down on "one," the downbeat. Gradually slow down and, without stopping, reverse direction. Start with left foot. Finish with a retard on the musical phrase, all arms held high, eyes looking up, both feet on half-toe.

"MEANDER" WITH EXIT

MUSIC AND TIME   Same as Basic Polka.

STARTING POSITION   After the conclusion of a circle polka, continue holding hands. A chosen leader releases and raises right arm high with hand free to gesture. All follow with Basic Polka.

DESCRIPTION   This is an exit pattern. The leader leads the circle into serpentine "meander loops" (see "Serpentine" in Glossary), or the movement can slow down sufficiently to create "through the needle" by dancing under any chosen arch, made by holding all arms very high while the polka is done almost in place. Give time for dancing around, down, forward, sideward—whatever pattern emerges, following the leader, to make it happen all together. The leader then leads the class off to exit, the last person holding on tightly with both hands together, in the manner of the children's game "Whip."

"BROTHER POLKA" FOR PARTNERS

(For ages ten and up)

MUSIC   Beethoven, "Contra Dances."

TIME   4/4; same as Basic Polka.

STARTING POSITION   Stand in a circle in pairs, facing partner; outside partner faces in to circle. Outside feet point in counterclockwise direction. Hold up inside hands higher than the head. Raise outside arms to shoulder height.

DESCRIPTION   To start, one Slide Polka with outside foot, face-to-face with partner. One Slide Polka with inside foot, turn back-to-back with partner, fingers of both inside hands held up lightly, look over shoulder at partner. Polka face-to-face and back-to-back three times (six measures). Keep the inside arms up high, bend the torso from side to side in direction of movement.

To continue, change: take four small skips to turn under arched arm. Return to start, stand high up on toes. Pause for musical phrase.

Continue this complete pattern for at least four times before finishing. Hands held high.

To extend polka pattern, continue to dance with the "Barrel Polka."

"BARREL POLKA"

MUSIC AND TIME   Same as "Brother Polka."

STARTING POSITION   Partners face-to-face, hands on each other's shoulders, elbows high out, outside foot extended and well pointed in counterclockwise direction.

DESCRIPTION   To prepare: mark four accents with pointed foot. Slide four slides in counterclockwise direction, then clockwise. Repeat each side four times.

To turn: keep arms on partners' shoulders. Look clockwise. Both partners take one polka sideward clockwise. Bend in the direction of circle. Make a half-turn to the right, polka with the other foot. Continue in the same direction of circle. Turn halfway around each time, with each polka to the side. Move around with the leading feet always stepping out together on the circle. Turn clockwise each polka step. Progress in the circle. To finish, take a deep breath. Raise both arms high.

DIONYSIAN

9

(For ages 12 or older)

A dramatic movement of the entire body inspired by Greek art and literature, and images depicted on vases and bas-reliefs showing the Dionysian rituals celebrating the wine festivals. It is a Bacchic dance movement. The head is tossed back in ecstasy, the chest is raised in an arch. The arms gesture thrusts a thyrsus into the ground to shake the rattle on top. The back leg is lifted with bent knee; each step thrust connects and disconnects from the earth.

MUSIC	None. Use breath phrases or drum beat.
TIME	6/8, slow; one completed movement for each six beats.
STARTING POSITION	Stand facing opposite corner, raise right arm in front to height of face. Raise left arm out in back. Palms in. Turn body onto diagonal line.
FLOOR PATTERN	Move diagonally from rear to front corner.
DESCRIPTION	Lift right knee forward, bend over knee. Hold right hand with dropped wrist over knee, left hand with wrist loose in back of hip (Figure 9.1a). Lower right foot with a light stamp. Step and small hop on right foot. Lift left leg in

77

9.1 *Dionysian.*

back. Push hips forward. Toss head way back, chin up, chest high. Thrust right hand down in front, palm and flexed wrist down. Keep right arm down in front, left arm down to the rear. Lift both wrists in front and back. Point index fingers down toward the earth (Figure 9.1b). Return left foot to the floor, release both arms down to the sides.

Image one: Bend forward, three counts: contract over to bring the right knee up in front again. Return to starting position, arms lifted front and rear. Stand on left foot.

Image two: Three counts: thrust right foot down to stamp on the floor, hop. Lift the left knee in back. Push hips forward. Toss the head back, push the chest up. Flex wrists down in front and back.

Repeat Dionysian thrust forward completely six times. Move toward the diagonal corner with every push forward. On the last movement, hold the chest lift arch with leg up in back. Change quickly, bend forward, place left knee on the floor. Fall back from the knee, release down to the floor. Move arm to bend back overhead, look up.

DANCE PATTERN WITH DIONYSIAN GESTURE

MUSIC   Schumann, "Happiness," from *Scenes from Childhood.*

TIME   2/4

STARTING POSITION   Start with right foot.

FLOOR PATTERN   From rear corner to diagonal front corner, then across front of dance space. Singly or in small groups, in turn.

DESCRIPTION   *measure one:* Start right foot run lightly four steps on diagonal forward. Lift both arms.

and: Raise right knee. Hop up on left foot.

measure two: make one Dionysian thrust on right foot down to stamp hop, lift left leg in back. Sustain full measure.

measure three: Spiral turn quickly to the right with four small steps on spot. Bring arms down then up overhead while turning in spiral.

measure four: Repeat quick spiral turn, with arms going down and up. Finish facing front, arms up.

measures five–six: Repeat entire action of measures one through four, with left foot and left hand, starting with left foot run across in front of dance space to the left corner.

measures seven–eight: Spiral turn left, twice, finish face front, arms up.

Return to starting place. Continue music until all have danced twice.

10

CHOREOGRAPHY FOR
YOUNG PEOPLE

In order to dance the choreography of Isadora Duncan, it is necessary to understand its relationship to the music. Not only does the music supply the emotional spur, but it also establishes the architecture of the dance pattern, without slavishly following it note by note. Once the framework of the pattern has been established, it is not necessary to count out phrases. Rather, it is important to listen and respond to the melodic line and the rhythmic beat for guidance. No matter how many times the dance is performed, it needs the freshness of the very first response. When the technical vocabulary is familiar, the body should be in tune to formulate the dance idea. The dance title given is for the purpose of indicating the content.

The gestures of the dance become the arm movements, which must spring from the solar plexus—the torso center—rather than from arbitrary, external arm placement. This body center will be the primary response to the music, then afterwards the gesture. The motor pattern of the feet, the locomotion, responds to the rhythmic pulse of the music. Both elements, the melodic and the rhythmic, have to coalesce with the torso to create the complete Duncan Dance. This, along with floor pattern and frontality, is essential for the success of communicating this art form and its messages, large or small. Yet everything must appear spontaneous—

the integral part of this choreographic legacy to pass on to new generations.

"LITTLE PARADE"

(For ages five to ten)

Dance pattern for eight children. The required movements are High Skip, Long Run, Stride.

MUSIC	Schumann, Soldier's March from "Album for the Young."
TIME	2/4, mark accents. Moderate tempo.
STARTING POSITION	Six children wait their turn at the left side of dance space. Two children, A and B, at separate rear corners.
DESCRIPTION	*measures one—four:* A and B skip eight High Skips separately from rear corners to opposite diagonal corners. Both start with left knee to right clenched fist (Figure 10.1a).
	measures five—eight: Both turn sharply at corner, cross over front of space with eight skips.
	measures nine—twelve: Both turn sharply at corner, take eight Long Runs diagonally.
	measures thirteen—sixteen: Turn, run eight Long Runs along rear.
	measures seventeen—twenty: Dancer A at left corner turns sharply and gestures to six to follow (Figure 10.1b).
	measures twenty-one—twenty-five: All march across rear of space with eight strides, single file. Swing the arms.
	measures twenty-six—twenty-eight: Turn corner, move in "serpentine" floor pattern for three changes of direction, eight Strides each.
	measures twenty-nine—thirty-two: Take four long steps forward, face front. Pause. All stand in two staggered lines, four children in front and four children interspaced in rear. Stamps measures thirty-one and thirty-two in place.

10.1 *"Little Parade."*

measures seventeen—thirty-two for dancer B: While the parade line has followed A, B in front marches in the opposite direction with three similar "serpentine" (see Glossary) bends (Figure 10.1b). After the third bend of the serpentine pattern (each takes eight steps across), B faces front, takes four steps forward to join the front line, at the side. B makes two stamps in place, on measures thirty-one and thirty-two. All are now facing the front.

MUSIC REPEATS FROM MEASURES SEVENTEEN TO THIRTY-TWO

measures seventeen—twenty-four: Strong accents—*count one:* back line rise on half-toe, stretch arms high overhead; front line make deep knee bend, hands on hips. *count two:* back line make deep knee bend; front line reach up.

Repeat up and downs four times in eight measures.

measure twenty-five: All charge forward diagonally, start on right foot, extend right arm forward, stretch left arm to the back.

measure twenty-six: Bring feet together sharply, arms down to sides.

measure twenty-seven: Lunge forward with left foot, right hand.

measure twenty-eight: Bring feet together, arms to sides.

measures twenty-nine—thirty-two: All stop. Reach both hands overhead. Fall flat to the right side, to finish.

"OVER THE SCARF"

(For six children ages six to eleven)

The required movements are High Skip, Fast Run, High Leap, Turning.

MUSIC — Schumann, Sicilienne from "Album for the Young" (Kalmus edition).

TIME — 6/8 (see note).

STARTING POSITION — Two children, A and B, stand opposite each other with space of two yards between in the center of the space at an angle. Raise scarf in both hands, right hand higher. Face clockwise, right shoulder to center. Rise high up on balls of feet, on the ready. Four children line up in left corner in order of entrance.

DESCRIPTION — *measures one–seven:* A and B hold scarf up overhead, look at each other, skip around twelve High Skips (two skips to each measure) to return to place at an angle to the entrance corner.

measures eight–nine: A and B kneel in starting place, scarf looped in right hand. Place right hand on knee, scarf dropped diagonally at an angle to the entrance. At the same time, first child of the four runs four fast runs into High Leap over the scarf on the accent (Figure 10.2).

Pause: Run two small steps after the leap to corner. Pause, look back, hands high.

MUSIC REPEATS: *measures one—nine:* A and B rise,

10.2 *"Over the Scarf."*

repeat skip around and kneel, while first child runs back to original corner, waving right hand, look back at scarf.

measures ten—seventeen: Second child skips back to entrance. Repeat same actions for third child, A and B.

Section two: *measures seventeen—twenty:* Third child skips back to entrance. Repeat same actions for fourth child, A and B. Fourth child runs to exit after pause.

measures twenty-eight—thirty-nine: A holds left hand high, scarf taut to waist in right hand. Turn continuously to the right, winding scarf into sash around waist. Reach and touch hand of B, standing. Turn left to unwind.

B repeats same action toward A.

Section one repeat: Da Capo to the end.

measures seventeen—twenty-four: A and B are in original places. Repeat twelve skips around with scarf held high overhead. Kneel with stretched scarf down low on diagonal, opposite entrance.

All four children run and leap together. Run a few steps, stop and look back.

After the music ends, A takes scarf in right hand, runs off with scarf held high. All chase after and run off.

Note: The leap accent is always on the strong fourth beat of the seventh measure. The complete pattern is: run, run, run, run and leap.

"ROUNDELAY"

(For all ages)

This is a "Ring Dance" improvisation. The required movements are Light Run, Swaying, and Calling Gestures.

MUSIC	Schumann, Roundelay from "Album for the Young."
TIME	6/8 legato.
STARTING POSITION	All stand in a circle, hold hands lightly.
DESCRIPTION	When the music begins rise high on half-toe, lift the arms up. Take a long breath. All drop weight to the right side, bend to the right, run lightly counterclockwise, swing the arms down. Bend the head in the direction of the circle.

The change of weight, arms dropping down and lifting up, creates a wavelike movement. Drop up and down four times for eight measures. Move chest and arms up high on the lift up. Pause at the crest of the lift each time.

After four lifts stop the circling, pause. One child is called out of the circle while the music continues. The designated child finds an arch made by the lifted arms of two previously decided children, bends under and runs through the arch to find a new circling place. The new leader turns to face the group and invents a gesture to call all to make a new circle. The group disbands, runs lightly, and reunites quickly with the leader. All take hands. Again the circle swings down and up four times. Pause again and name a new leader to find another circling place.

The students learn to use mime and to respond quickly as a group. If the class is large, each lesson should use only a few leaders. Eventually all should have a turn to lead.

"UNDER THE SCARF"

(For nine dancers, mixed ages)

The required movement is the Waltz.

MUSIC Schubert's Waltz op. 33, no. 12

TIME 3/4. With repeat. Marcato lyrical.

STARTING POSITION In the center of space two dancers, preferably tall, stand in profile, facing each other and holding firmly the ends of a long, light silk scarf (three yards long, one yard wide). Hold the scarf folded in so that the belly of the drape touches the floor. Stand with feet together, eyes and head down. Hands down.

Seven dancers stand along the rear wall in relaxed groupings. Stand at ease holding hands with each other. Each moves up to be ready at the center in turn, in this order: one single, one single, two as partners, three as an image of "Three Graces" (Figure 10.3). Scarf repeats the same action each time, every eight measures.

SECTION A

measure one: Scarf dancers count "and," lift right knee high in front of body to prepare scarf. Bring belly of scarf up by lifting, with arms going high and wrists flexing. On "one," step forward on right foot as arms go up, small hop. Arch chest, lift head, push left knee high up in back. Hold arc of scarf with arched back for "two-and-three," arms high. Return left foot to floor.

10.3 *"Under the Scarf."*

measures two—six: Waltz step in place as scarf descends very slowly.

measures seven—eight: Return scarf to fold position, belly down; bring hands together, feet together.

AT THE SAME TIME:
Repeat music A.

measures one—two: First dancer in center of line face front, from center of line dance forward with four Basic Waltz steps toward the scarf. Bring arms down and cross, look down.

measures three—four: Arms uncross, look up at scarf, lift arms out.

measures five—six: Balancé Waltz, right foot forward, look right; left foot back, look left. Arms shoulder height.

measures seven—eight: Bend over, run to the right around scarf to last position in the line.

MUSIC REPEAT SECTION A:

measures one—eight: Second dancer same as first, but run to the left around scarf to the end of line.

MUSIC SECTION B:

measures nine—sixteen: Two dancers from center of line, hold right hands in "guiding" position, do four running waltzes, starting with right foot. Partner on left turns under own right arm. Partner on right turns under own right arm. Release hands, separate, run right and left around scarf, return to end of the line.

MUSIC REPEAT SECTION B:

measures nine—fourteen: Three dancers in "Three Graces" position, tallest preferably in the center, holding outside hands of two dancers (see Figure 10.3), waltz forward four Basic Waltz steps, starting with right foot.

measures fifteen—sixteen: Lift arms forward, look up under the scarf. Release hands. Center dancer runs back under the scarf, outside dancers run around scarf to ends of lines.

MUSIC RETURN SECTION A:

measures one—six: All seven dancers dance forward under the scarf in a loose group, "Three Graces" center figure in middle. Six Basic Waltz steps forward under and through the arc of the scarf. Do not stop under the scarf. Arms cross down and uncross up. All look up at scarf.

measures seven—eight: Three dancers run to the right, around the scarf; three dancers run to the left around scarf. Center dancer runs back under scarf to center.

All quickly join hands at rear of space, lift arms high in a line. Scarf is held stretched full length across, waist-high in outside hands of outer figures.

MUSIC REPEAT SECTION A:

measure one: Dancers in the line face front, Waltz Balancé forward with right foot. All look right.

measure two: Balancé Waltz back with left foot. Look left.

measures three—six: Balancé Waltz forward and back, right and left foot. Repeat.

measure seven: All run forward, bend body against scarf, arms up.

measure eight: Hold arms up higher, stand on half-toe. Look up.

AT THE SAME TIME

measure one: Scarf holders waltz to the line. Move scarf up to line at waist height.

measure two: Waltz away from line. Move scarf away.

measure three: Step waltz to the line. Move scarf in.

measure four: Waltz away from the line. Move scarf away.

measure five: Waltz to the line. Move scarf in.

measure six: Hold scarf down against line, waist-high and stretched to the fullest.

measures seven—eight: All line and scarf dancers run quickly forward, scarf stretched waist-high.

All lift arms up. Lift scarf high on last note. Hold.

After the music ends, one chosen dancer takes the scarf, runs with it high in the air in a circle, then exits with a high leap. All the others follow and exit after the scarf.

"THE CRADLE LULLABY"

(For all ages)

This dance is subtle in the dramatic changes required. In the first part, to music A, the gesture demands quiet from unseen noisy sources. In the second or B part, the gesture collects all the music from birds and trees to sing the infant to sleep and protect it. "Remember, Mother is always here," it says. Perhaps the song "Flow Gently Sweet Afton" summons the same images in song. This dance has a very lyrical quality to express. Be sure the chest always moves before the arms or legs. The required movement is the Balancé Waltz.

MUSIC   Schubert's waltz; *Deutsche Tänz* no. 12.

TIME   3/4. Lento, expressivo. A repeat, B repeat, A repeat, B repeat

STARTING POSITION   Solo or group: stand in center, look down, weight on left foot.

MUSIC A

measure one: One waltz step to the right side with right foot, on half-toes. Swing both arms down and over to the right, shoulder height. Look down at the floor over left shoulder. This creates a cradle rocking (Figure 10.4a).

measure two: One waltz step to the left side with left foot, on half-toes. Swing both arms down and over to the left, shoulder height. The hands make smoothing gestures with bent wrists patting.

measure three: One waltz step to the right, look out to the right, turn face to side. Lift right hand

10.4 *"Cradle Lullaby."*

up, bring index finger to the lips (hush) (Figure 10.4b).

measure four: One waltz step to the left, look out to the left, turn face to left side. Bring left hand with index finger to the lips (hush).

measures five—six: Repeat rocking Balancé Waltz, as in measures one and two.

measure seven: Bring right hand with index finger to the lips, look to the right.

measure eight: Step right, stand still in position, move index finger out to the right side. Bend to the direction of the hand gesture (hush).

MUSIC A REPEAT

Repeat measures one through eight, rocking and hushing gestures.

MUSIC B:

measure nine: Waltz forward on right foot, lift chest, arms out, look way up. Both arms swing up high and out at the sides, hands mark the music lightly (Figure 10.4c).

measure ten: Waltz backward on left foot, lower chest, look down at center. Both arms swing down and out, stay at shoulder height, curve over forward. Look down at the cradle (Figure 10.4d).

measures eleven—twelve: Repeat action of measures nine and ten. Rock up and down, arms out to the sides.

measures thirteen—fourteen: Tiptoe six small steps in a circle counterclockwise. Left hand palm down into center, look down at the child in the cradle. Right hand out to the side.

measures fifteen—sixteen: Stand still, arms out. Keep looking down (Is the child asleep?). Let the body respond to the question (Not yet).

MUSIC B REPEAT

measures nine—sixteen: Repeat the action of rocking up and down, circling.

RETURN TO MUSIC A

measures one—eight: Repeat actions of cradle and hush.

RETURN TO MUSIC B

measures nine—sixteen: Repeat action of rocking.

MUSIC B REPEAT

measure nine: Waltz forward on right foot, lift chest very high, look up. Swing both arms up and out to side, fingers mark the music.

measure ten: Waltz backward on left foot, lower chest, look down at center. Swing both arms down to hips, curve body over and forward.

measures eleven—twelve: Repeat action of measures nine and ten (feel as if singing a lullaby).

measure thirteen: Step forward with right foot, look down, lift left knee, toes extended down in front.

measure fourteen: Take a deep breath, relevé on right foot, stay on half-toe, arms out to sides, shoulder height.

measure fifteen: Gently place left foot down, kneel on right knee. Both arms around and down in a gesture of picking up an infant.

measure sixteen: Fold both arms over knee in a cradle gesture. Bend head over to the left side. Look down at infant with love. Hold the image (Figure 10.4e)!

NOTES FOR THE TEACHER 〜

THE CLASS ROUTINE

The Duncan schools were the first to create a kind of leotard to allow the body to be unconstrained and visibly accountable. The first part of the lesson is in such body suits, preferably in a light color. Drapes and tunics are helpful to heighten drama and create escape from the ordinary; short light jersey or silky tunics are attractive. Little wreaths and headbands for occasions are lovely. A class might feel connected if all wear one color. Bare legs and feet should be insisted upon. Students need to be encouraged to feel that they are entering a beautiful experience when they come into the dance space. They are expected to be the best of themselves.

Everyone is making a special effort to observe all instructions. No gum-chewing or loud talking. Even sitting down on the floor to await a turn is done in one manner: Kneel on one knee, sit to that side, lean and rest on hand, bring both knees together, feet out to the far side. To rise from that position, return to the knee, stand up, and be ready.

Familiar class routines at the beginning and end of class help define demands more easily. Duncan classes usually begin with barre work for stretching and limbering. After this, there are the chosen basic movements, followed by "center" for slow movements. Some improvisation or working on Duncan choreography might follow. Class usually closes with the "grand polka." Sometimes there is a unified closed, embracing circle, holding onto our dance companions in a fond, friendly farewell—a "Thank you." At other times there is a more theatrical exit, such as dancing the polka, all in a long meandering line—circling and looping, holding hands behind the leader—changed each lesson—all exit and dancing a "Reigen."

IMPROVISATION SUGGESTIONS

The Duncan technique itself includes the opportunity to improvise while learning. For instance, in dancing the Skip, which emphasizes free movement and strong elevation, the dynamics change from large to small movements. The arms and hands, while following the melodic line, create an imaginary scene with gestures to unseen comrades, to growing plants on earth, to sun and sky. The Skip is the basis for an impromptu dance about relationships to the world.

Or apply this to a specific piece of music chosen to create patterns evoked by the form of the music. The student learns to start and stop on the musical phrase. One student starts listening for phrases, dancing alone, then finds a new phrase and chooses a partner to dance together, then finds a phrase to bid farewell, and finally leaves the second dancer alone to find the phrases. There emerges a solo, a duet, a new solo, which will continue the patterns. Schubert waltzes are very suitable for this play dance.

For younger children there should be story improvisations, which can be worked out at home. The teacher can assign roles in class from popular musical tales, such as Prokofiev's *Peter and the Wolf* or Mendelssohn's *Midsummer Night's Dream*. In class, the Nocturne from *Midsummer Night's Dream* is a favorite. One child, as the Queen, slowly lies down to sleep. The others sit at her feet. Each child then dances a mime dance of picking flowers, covering the Queen, and lying down gently beside her. When all the children are lying down, the Queen wakes as the morning comes. She wakes the others without a sound; they all run and disappear, "away, away."

"I have no system," Isadora was reported to have said when asked about the method of instruction in her schools.

What I have found in teaching Isadora Duncan's concept of dancing and in preparing this book is the rediscovery that her school of dance provides a most natural learning process for young people. What they learn, coupled with a sensitivity to all the arts and humanities, creates that ideal harmony for strengthening both the inner and outer selves.

The method is in the learning of the movement itself.

GLOSSARY

Amazon A mythological Greek strong feminist prototype.

Beinschwingen A German word meaning "leg bone swings." Used for barre work in the dance classes of Isadora, her sister Elizabeth, and their pupils.

Dionysian Bacchic movement from Greek wine festival.

Figure-Eight Floor pattern used in Duncan choreography and classwork, based on the figure-eight configuration: from left to right across diagonal and around front and rear.

Focus Body and face in line with eyes and chin in the direction of the movement or gesture.

Frontality Awareness of the line of the body to front of the dance space and audience. Based on bas-reliefs from ancient Egyptian and Greek art.

Grip Lock Used to grip hands in a circle. Every other person turns palm up. Holding hands palm to palm, slip thumb and forefinger around wrist and pinky.

Hop-Skip Swing step (in German, *Hupfenschwingen*). A dance-step combination of hop forward and skip up. Hips move forward on accent of hop.

Panathenaic Greek festival procession, young people bearing gifts to Athena.

Phalanx Group movement maintaining individual space relationship.

Reigen Isadora recalling the circling dances, perhaps the Polka. Apparently a very happy part of the children's classwork in the Duncan schools (from "A Letter to the Pupils," from *The Art of the Dance* by Isadora Duncan).

Serpentine A floor pattern used in Duncan choreography and classwork. Winding through space and suggestive of a serpent's meander in a wide zig-zag from front to rear or vice versa.

Solar Plexus (Center) Isadora Duncan referred to the solar plexus as the radial center from which all motion emanates. Located physically in the front of the chest under the ribs, it is the diaphragm muscle that is responsible for breathing and responsive to emotional stimuli. It contracts to negative feelings, pain or fear, and expands with the positive, joy or love. This "center" must activate the dance with both locomotive and gestural

97

movements in order for the dance to appear genuine and communicative.

"Tanagra Figures" A series of slow-motion studies for legato and equilibrium. Based on small Greek terra-cotta figurines showing daily life motifs. Also reflects images of movement in Renaissance paintings of Greek myths.

Turnout Position of the feet and knees, usually a "V" form for the feet heels in, toes out. Knees are rotated out from the hips. Turnout is customary, unless otherwise stated.

Unpointed "pointed toe" In all the Duncan footwork the toes are extended, but not overly pointed. Arch the foot, extend the ankle as much as possible, but leave the toes relaxed enough to let the foot make contact with the floor and be ready for the rebound. The ball of the toes will be prepared to receive the weight and push up quickly.

Weaving Floor pattern for two dancers, taking turns in holding back and rushing forward as they change places at the corners. (Figure G.1)

G.1 *Weaving*

OF RELATED INTEREST

ISADORA DUNCAN DANCE: Technique and Repertory performed by the Isadora Duncan Dance Ensemble directed by Julia Levien and Andrea Mantell Seidel

A demonstration of the technique of Isadora Duncan staged by Julia Levien followed by performances or original Duncan repertory between 1905 and 1923, directed by Andrea Mantell Seidel. Chronologically arranged, they include the buoyant SOUTHERN ROSES (Johann Strauss); Schubert and Chopin waltzes; dances from the Gluck operas; and the Russian revolutionary dances, VARSHIVIANKA and DUBINUSHKA. Also includes an historical introduction to Duncan's technique and the development of her schools, as well as interviews and commentary by Levien, Seidel, members of the Company, and Daniel Lewis, Dean of Dance, New World School of the Arts, Miami, FL.

Julia Levien *performed in the companies of Anna and Irma Duncan of the original Duncan School. She teaches in New York and Miami and has given workshops and lectures at many educational institutions in the U.S. and abroad. She is the author of* **DUNCAN DANCE: A GUIDE FOR YOUNG PEOPLE AGES SIX TO SIXTEEN.**

Andrea Mantell Seidel *holds a Doctor of Arts in dance from New York University, is Assistant Professor of Dance at the New World School of the Arts and Florida International University, and has studied and performed Duncan dance with Lori Belilove and Julia Levien since 1981.*

60 minutes (color), 1994, $49.95

Book

THE SEARCH FOR ISADORA: The Legend and Legacy of Isadora Duncan by Lillian Loewenthal

Rather that rehashing the well-known facts of Isadora's life, this book presents new information for reappraising her significance as one of the most influential figures of the twentieth century in dance, art, fashion, education and women's liberation. Author Lillian Loewenthal visited the places associated with Isadora and interviewed those who knew her personally. Loewenthal profiles Isadora's best-known discipiles, known collectively as "The Isadorables."

Lillian Loewenthal *is an authority on Isadora Duncan. She served as archivist for the Isadora Duncan Centennial.*

240 pages, 50 photos and drawings, hardbound, $26.95
ISBN 0-87127-179-6

O R D E R   F O R M

Please send me:

☐ Isadora Duncan Dance: Technique and Repertory $49.95

☐ The Search for Isadora $26.95

Name _____

Address _____

City _____ State _____ ZIP _____

Day Phone _____

☐ My check or money order for $ _____ is enclosed.

☐ Please charge: ☐ Visa   ☐ MasterCard   ☐ American Express

Account Number _____ Exp. Date _____

Signature_____

☐ Please send your FREE dance book and video catalog.

You may phone in your order from
8:30 - 4:30 Eastern time at our toll-free number
1-800-220-7149

Return this form with your payment to:
Princeton Book Company, Publishers
PO Box 57
Pennington, New Jersey 08534